D 40

DEATH WHERE IS YOUR STING?

DEATH
WHERE IS YOUR STING?

by

George A. Maloney, S.J.

ALBA · HOUSE   NEW · YORK

SOCIETY OF ST. PAUL, 2187 VICTORY BLVD., STATEN ISLAND, NEW YORK 10314

Library of Congress Cataloging in Publication Data

Maloney, George A., 1924-
   Death, where is your sting?

   1. Future life. 2. Death—Religious aspects—
Christianity. I. Title.
BT902.M35   1984   236'.2   84-9216
ISBN 0-8189-0470-4

Imprimi Potest:
Vincent M. Cooke, S.J.
Provincial, New York Province

Designed, printed and bound in the United States of
America by the Fathers and Brothers of the
Society of St. Paul, 2187 Victory Boulevard,
Staten Island, New York 10314, as part of their
communications apostolate.

4 5 6 7 8 9 (Current Printing: first digit).

Contents

Acknowledgments

Sincere thanks to Mrs. Rita Ruggiero for typing the manuscript and to Sister Joseph Agnes, S.C.H. for her careful reading and correcting of the manuscript and other suggestions that proved most helpful.

Dedication

To Janet Morton and John Ryan
who believe in miracles

Introduction

What style of preaching, what sort of message, what kind of teaching would Jesus proclaim today were He to return in human form and meet us in our modern setting? He would surely adapt His approach to the culture of our time, so different from that of His Jewish contemporaries two thousand years ago. But what about the substance of His message? What is there in the Gospel that is true and relevant for all times and for all human beings everywhere on the face of the earth?

Four pivotal elements in Jesus' proclamation of God's gift of eternal life come to mind. First of all, Jesus would undoubtedly announce clearly today, as He did to His Palestinian listeners, that the Kingdom of God, the Kingdom of living in the experience of the trinitarian community's love for us, is always breaking in upon us personally and individually. God— Father, Son and Holy Spirit—is always personally present to us, filling us with His self-giving, uncreated energy of love. Entrance into that Kingdom relationship brings about in our relationships not only with God but with ourself, our neighbors and the entire universe a peace, joy and sense of harmonious unity in our personal oneness and yet uniqueness, so different and free from the individuality and uniqueness of other creatures.

Secondly, Jesus would surely tell us that there is an urgency at this very moment in our "enlightened" 20th century for us to wake up from our hypnotic sleep and arise from the world of the dead to receive the light of Christ. Though we are born physically after nine months of extended sleep in our mother's womb, yet we continue to live all too often in a world of dreamy darkness. We live in a psychic and spiritual sleep. Most of us dwell in a world different from God's true and real world. The great deception is that we do not realize that we are asleep to God's reality because our false egos have constructed around us a world of illusion. Even "religion," our own interpretation of God's revealed truths found in Scripture and in the teachings of the Church, can help to keep us locked into our self-created world.

Jesus approaches us in our daily life and finds us asleep, enjoying our dreams, our fanciful imaginations of what we perceive to be reality. "He came back to the disciples and found them sleeping . . ." (Mt 26:40). He is ready to wake us up as He did Lazarus: "Our friend Lazarus is resting. I am going to wake him" (Jn 11:11).

Thirdly, He would certainly insist on our need for conversion, a conversion that is characterized by a real upheaval in our lives, an embracing of the cross, a dying to the unreal world of our own fabrication if we are to enter into God's Kingdom. The seed must die before it can bring forth new and more abundant life (Jn 12:24). If we wish to live in God's real world of loving harmony, we must be ready to deny ourselves the satisfaction of our illusory desires (Ep 4:22) and to die to our "old self" in order to find our true life (Mk 8:35).

Fourthly, Jesus would without question renew His personal invitation to each of us individually to share more abundantly in His new and eternal life (Jn 10:10; 11:25-26). Thomas Merton writes:

> The only true joy on earth is to escape from the prison of our own false self, and enter by love into union with the Life Who dwells and sings within the essence of every creature and in the core of our own souls. In His love we possess all things and enjoy fruition of them, finding Him in them all.[1]

CALL TO DECISION

There have been many books recently published about life after death. Among those books I humbly include one written by me: *The Everlasting Now.*[2] But after speaking often before Christian audiences about this subject, I saw the need to write a book that would take the truth about life after death, as revealed by God and found in Scripture and the Church's constant teaching through the ages, and present them as practical meditations that would stir the reader to an urgent decision.

Most of us Christians, I believe, give an intellectual assent to the truths about our own physical death, about Purgatory, Heaven and Hell, about our ability to pray for our beloved departed and the intercessory power of the communion of the Saints. We believe in our own individual bodily resurrection from the dead at the end of the world. Yet we usually place such truths in *time* and *place* categories in the nebulous future so that the impact of Jesus' call to a *now* decision to begin living in His eternal life has little urgency for us.

DEATH-RESURRECTION NOW!

I have presented these truths about the life that awaits us after our death and the death of our loved ones in a process view. God shares His likeness with each one of us by bestowing upon us the godly power of free will. This is the divine fire planted within our hearts by which we can freely accept God's infinite love or freely disdain His humble offer.

If we freely wish to remain in our darkness and refuse to accept the light of Christ, we, even now, create a world that is unreal. God does not know this world. We have created it by ourselves. We set up a world of disharmony, chaos and utter disorder. We worship ourselves as God, the beginning and end of the world we have created. But because God has nothing to do with the unreality of our false self, that world has no true existence.

The more we choose to live according to this false self, the deeper we move away from God's real world and freely lock ourselves in an inescapable prison of selfishness. Sartre claimed others were Hell. But Hell is our own creation and we are our own judges and prosecutors. We turn through sin from life and live in death. We unceasingly insist that God and the world of His Saints are false and only our world is true, causing ourselves more pain yet.

Every time we listen to the indwelling Word of God leading us into His light by challenging us to let go of our selfish ego and our unreal world and to take the risk to live in love, we begin to enter here and now in this life into a share of God's Kingdom of Heaven. Realizing that Heaven is living already by God's grace and our cooperation, according to God's "truth and love" (Ep 4:15), we accept the exciting journey of an eternal life of growing into seeing Christ in all things and all things in Him (Col 3:11). What a difference in our daily choices to act on the faith that our eternal happiness in Heaven is being determined now by our dynamic living out of our death to selfishness and our rising to a new oneness in the risen Christ.

The resurrection of our bodies is not something that is put off into the far future of the end of the world but it is a choice we are freely asked by the indwelling, risen Christ to make now. Our deceased loved ones can be helped and healed as we unite our love for them with the healing power of Christ as He extends Himself to us in His Church.

Those same loved ones can be present to us as we believe that they truly live with all the love relationships they had with us while they were on this earth.

In a word, the truths revealed to us by Christ through His Church about life after death are gifts of grace calling us to assert our precious God-given free will to live in each thought, word and deed in love. For love freely given by us has the gentle power to span all distances, all times and to conquer the seeming abyss that separates us on earth from those who have passed beyond the grave into eternal life. The love of God that abounds in our hearts through the Spirit that is given to us (Rm 5:5) is what takes away from death all sting and all victory (1 Cor 15:55).

I have added a prayer at the end of each chapter to involve the reader in a faith presence to God to pray out the truth developed in each chapter. May such suggested prayers and insights encourage the reader to move deeper into the experience Jesus intended His followers to have. He announced the Good News as breaking in *now* upon all who hear and receive His Word as good earth, well prepared and waiting eagerly, to accept His saving message which will continuously bring forth new life unto a hundredfold.

Our future, eternal life is being given to us now in the awesome importance of this present moment. May this book help each one of us to act on the words of Scripture:

> Wake up from your sleep,
>   rise from the dead,
> and Christ will shine on you (Ep 5:14).

George A. Maloney, S.J.

August 15, 1983
Feast of Our Lady's Assumption

Footnotes

1. Thomas Merton, *New Seeds of Contemplation* (N.Y.: New Direction Books, 1962), p. 25.
2. G.A. Maloney, S.J., *The Everlasting Now* (Notre Dame, IN.: Ave Maria Press, 1980).

DEATH
WHERE IS YOUR STING?

CHAPTER ONE

MY LOVED ONE HAS DIED, NOW WHAT?

She rushed into his hospital room. Her eyes went immediately to the bed of her husband. But from the look on his face and on the face of the two nurses and the doctor, she knew that she had arrived too late. Her husband was dead! My younger brother had died at the relatively early age of 54.

Charmion, his wife, held his cold hand. He seemed all right last night when she left him. And now he was gone forever! Now what? That question hit her with the force of a tornado that seemingly sucked out her very breath from deep within.

"Why, God? Why did you take him? He was still too young to die. And now, how am I going to manage without him? There's the funeral to arrange. Relatives and friends to call." Red-hot flashes sear her brain like branding iron on an animal skin, filling her whole being with thoughts and memories of how she lost her father when she was a small girl, of the happy moments spent with her husband and children. And then the shuddering, icy reality would pass into her consciousness: death snatches away loved ones and never gives them back!

Never, never again will she see her loved one, her husband. Depression fills her with choking sobs as she contemplates the long future, so empty, so alone. Then a feeling of standing on rubbery legs, an inability to walk forward into that future.

"What meaning is there left to my life without him? We had so many plans when he would have retired. And now?"

The bubble burst but with a bang that set up new explosions in her heart—anger toward God, toward the doctors, regret that she encouraged him to have the operation. She reached out to God, her constant strength in trials of the past. But her hands touched nothing but silent, empty air! "God, I need you! Why don't you do something? Come and help me in my need! Don't you see how confused I am and hurting?" It is as if she were banging on a huge steel door. God is safely sleeping inside and He has locked the entrance and even bolted it for good measure!

Then guilt, like a squirming snake, crawls out from hidden areas of her mind to spit venom at her for the times she did not love her husband as she should have. What physical pain he must have been suffering as she chided him for being a hypochondriac! And the times he needed loving but she felt too tired to be bothered. "Oh, for one more chance to tell him how much I care for him!" But now there will be no more chances.

It's over, she thought. He will never answer her plea, "Come back." He has passed over into the beyond. His boat has passed out into the dark ocean, leaving her alone on the shore. He is out of sight. Now there are only memories of what was and of what she would have wanted.

But what about him? Where did he go? When his ship anchors in his new land, what will he be like? Could they possibly get in touch with each other? Are there telephones there so she can call from time to time? Will he miss her and the children?

DEATH, THE REAPER

All of us have experienced the passing of a loved one. Perhaps the most recent encounter we had with Death, the

Reaper, who always wins out, was when we lost a husband, wife, mother or father. Perhaps we recently buried a son or daughter, a brother or sister or some other relative we loved. We all have felt the permanent absence of a very dear friend.

No one can lessen the pain of loss, the wrenching of someone out of our heart to be there no more as they were at one time when they were so much a part of our life. Grief is important and part of a necessary healing process to re-condition us to *reality*.

But precisely what is that new, real world in which we must now live in regard to our beloved departed one? Perhaps our Christian faith can change our attitudes toward the loss of a loved one and bring us into a truer picture of things as they really are in God's world, the way He sees things and the way, therefore, we should want to live.

More than any other human experience on earth, death brings us into ultimate concern. We are forced in the most powerful way to destroy all our idols. God calls us deeper into the humility of learning that we are not the center of reality, but He alone is. Our tinker toy constructions of reality come falling down as we are challenged by God to enter into a deeper grasp of His vision of reality. Unfortunately our very Christian religion has all too often given us a faulty vision of death.

DEATH, THE INVADING ENEMY

For sure, the way we have accepted what we have thought to be a Christian understanding of death makes it impossible to see death as anything but negative. We are brought up to want life. Death opposes life. It is an alien invader that should not be present on planet Earth. Our reading of the Book of Genesis as a history book and not a faith revelation from God implies that the ideal man without sin would never have had to die. Death is the wages of sin.

Sin, man's turning away from God, brought, in this view, God's wrathful punishment to earth and thereafter every man, woman and child would have to taste the terrifying sting of death's victory over them. Some Christian teachers have confused us even more and taken us farther away from facing the reality of death as a necessary and normal part of human development. Teachings on the immortality of the soul and the immortal, resurrected body at the end of the world have tended to mollify us. The result has been that we do not take death seriously as a part of human growth, a part of greater life.

A MORE ANCIENT VIEW

In the early Christian Church, especially among some of the Eastern Fathers, there was a theological teaching based on Scripture to which many modern theologians are returning[1] that sees actual, physical death, not as a punishment for sin, but creatively, as a part of being human. If death were not considered as a punishment for sin but as part of the total evolution of the human person toward the sharing of God's freely offered gift of His trinitarian life, would not such an understanding of death change our attitude toward our deceased loved ones? Would we not learn how to live more humanly now by believing that our daily, "deathly" encounters with the idols we create to build a false immortality for ourselves even now bring us into a greater sharing in God's eternal life?

MORE ABUNDANT LIFE

Jesus came among us that we might share more abundantly in God's life (Jn 10:10).

I am the resurrection.
If anyone believes in me, even though he dies he will live,
and whoever lives and believes in me
will never die.
Do you believe this? (Jn 11:25-26)

He sought to lead His followers into the truth that God alone is to be adored. There can be no false gods before the one, true God. But to live in God's truth, His reality, all human beings must face a dying to possessiveness, to being their own god.

> Anyone who prefers father or mother to me is not worthy of me. Anyone who prefers son or daughter to me is not worthy of me. Anyone who does not take his cross and follow in my footsteps is not worthy of me. Anyone who finds his life will lose it; anyone who loses his life for my sake will find it (Mt 10:37-39).

And yet, how slowly we mature in our daily opportunities to die to the independent control we wish to exercise over our own lives! How important it is that we see death as a most necessary teacher when we lose a loved one who has become a vital part of our lives! The greatest lessons in life come to us when we face our own death and the final shattering of the illusion that we could ever live without total dependence upon God's love and His gift of life.

Death has everything to do with our becoming the human beings God has called us to become when "He chose us, chose us in Christ, to be holy and spotless, and to live through love in His presence . . ." (Ep 1:4). It is in Christ's death that we obtain eternal life. It is in dying that we live. It is in the death of husband, wife and all our needed loved ones that God calls us to rise from the shattered ruins of the false idols we constructed around our so-called loved ones in order truly to love them in a new and more godly manner.

DEATH BRINGS NEW LIFE

What sin brings to death is an accumulation of all our fears and guilt that prevents us from trusting in God's power to give life through death. We intellectually give an assent to the belief that our loved ones truly live after they depart from us, bereaving their earthly absence. But God wants us to *really* believe they truly are alive and when we die we too will live eternally.

At the moment of our earthly demise, we and our loved ones enter into a new life beyond death. If this is true, does this truth operate daily in our attitude toward our departed loved ones? Do we really believe that they live with the same consciousness we were able to share with them before death?

Scripture is rather strongly against conjuring up the spirits of the dead. Saul went to the necromancer of Endor, a caller of dead spirits, to receive knowledge and power, not from God but from a diabolical force (1 S 28:3-25). But God's revelation, through the Church's constant teaching and liturgical practice of praying for the dead, shows us that there can be a wholesome communication in love that takes away the sting and victory of death (1 Cor 15:55) and allows us to be channels of God's healing love toward those who reach out from beyond this vale of tears to love us with God's very own love in them.

DEATHLY IDOLS

In ministering to bereaving Christians I have often met a very unhealthy attitude toward their recently departed loved ones. One woman for several years after the death of her husband would daily enter into her bedroom closet and touch the suits and shirts, pants and shoes of her dead husband. She was bowing before an idol that she had created out of the past to feed her own self-centered needs. She was refusing to accept

God's truth that her husband still lives and that she should enter into that reality by sacrificing her "golden calf" and move on deeper into the desert of life to meet God on His terms.

In his classic on bereavement, *A Grief Observed*, C.S. Lewis shares with us a most important truth which he arrived at through his anguish at the death of his wife. Through the application of his Christian faith he came to realize in his grief that death allowed him to love, not only his wife, but also God in a deeper manner and with a purer motive, removed from any idol-casting of the one he loved in such a rich though manipulative kind of way.

He found that the more he forgot himself with all the "phantasmagoria" which he had created to keep his wife more dead and turned to God in humble faith, the more he came into a loving communion with his wife. He writes:

> And suddenly at the very moment when, so far, I mourned H. [his deceased wife] least, I remembered her best. Indeed it was something (almost) better than memory; an instantaneous, unanswerable impression. To say it was like a meeting would be going too far. Yet there was that in it which tempts one to use those words. It was as if the lifting of the sorrow removed a barrier.[2]

LIVING FAITH

What is the secret of communing with our departed loved ones? Our relationships with them are very similar to our loving relationships with God. We are commanded by God not to make any false gods out of the living God of Abraham, Isaac and Jacob. We are not to come into His presence to exploit God for our own selfish purposes. We cannot remember and love God enough. We are to pray incessantly (1 Th 5:17).

So with our beloved, departed ones we are to love them unceasingly but unselfishly in the love of God. We are to uproot any clinging to them in our "controlled" way and to enter into a faith-relationship with them that goes far beyond any so-called "feeling." We seek the presence of our beloved by offering ourselves in loving service to do all we can to make them eternally happy.

THE DEAD ARE ALIVE

The first act of faith which we need to exercise daily is to believe that our beloved one is truly alive, the very same person with all the memories, joys and sorrows we both experienced in our earthly life together. We need to wipe away an understanding of death as a separation of our beloved's body from the soul. St. Paul teaches us with his holistic view of the human being, that we are whole persons not made up of separable parts, yet having distinct levels of relationships as "spirit, soul and body" (1 Th 5:23). Our beloved, the whole person, has died. Yet the whole person still lives. He/she is as alive as Christ is consciously the center of his/her life.

That whole person, the biblical *soma*, body-person or embodied human being, is now after death more cosmically open to the whole universe. The one we love upon death has become "all-cosmic," to use Karl Rahner's expression.[3] Death has brought an end to our loved one's immersion in a lower stage of evolutionary development, the vegetable and animal level. Such a one through death moves higher in God's creative love to a greater complexity-in-consciousness where he/she now relates in greater intensity to the cosmic world, including new relationships to us, through an expanding awareness of solidarity, both harmonious and disharmonious, with us and the entire material world while also attaining a new realization of his/her unique being in relationship to God.

LOVE ENDURES FOREVER

The second area of faith-exercise on our part is to live often through the day or night in the loving presence of our beloved. It is not "spooky" to commune and, therefore, to speak to the dead, for they are as alive, and even more alive, as we are. If at one time our loved ones reached out to us in love and found new self-dignity through the love that we once gave them, why do we doubt that our love is eagerly sought for by our departed loved ones now?

It is love, God's love in us that becomes perfected (1 Jn 4:12) when we love both the living and the dead, for they are all alive in Christ through the Spirit that begets such love. Blessed Robert Southwell, S.J., the English martyr of the 16th century, beautifully expresses this truth: "Not where I breathe do I live, but where I love."

LOVE HEALS

Thirdly, by our loving remembrance of our beloved deceased ones, we have the power to bring Christ's healing to them. This has been the conviction of the Church in encouraging Christians through all centuries to make sacrifices, offer alms, prayers and, above all, to have the Divine Liturgy offered on behalf of the departed.

If we could pray for those loved ones while they lived on earth, the Church assures us that we can make contact with our departed and, through our prayers united to the powerful intercession of Jesus, the High Priest, we can help them in their new existence after their death. This is seen in the ancient practice kept alive in the Byzantine Liturgy of St. John Chrysostom of praying for all types of human beings, those living and those who have passed beyond this earth, both the saints and the sinners. For Christians united in Christ there is a union between the various states of the Body of Christ, the Church, militant, suffering and triumphant. All believing Christians in love can bring the healing love of Christ to others, regardless of what form of existence in Christ they are now found.

Realistically speaking we know the need for further healing that our loved ones who have gone before us into eternal life have. There is no human being who is not in need of greater love, both divine and human, to bring about a healing of the brokenness and many hurts received in relationships while he or she lived on earth. As these hurts came through relationships with others, they can be healed only in the context of the community of believers in Christ who remember their loved ones and sacrifice themselves out of love for the deceased.

St. Paul prayed for the dead Onesiphorus: "May it be the Lord's will that he shall find the Lord's mercy on that Day" (2 Tm 1:18). Baruch prayed: "Do not call to mind the misdeeds of our ancestors, but remember instead your power and your name" (Ba 3:5). We can help our beloved ones as we pray for them, especially in the context of the Liturgy, and offer sacrifices conceived out of love. The love that released the infinite love of Christ for the beloved deceased depends upon our "consociating" with Christ by putting on His mind. The more we offer liturgies and prayers and sacrifices for the deceased and surrender ourselves to Christ by expressing love for our beloved departed as one with the love of Christ, the greater will be the healing they will receive through the merits of Christ.

The Liturgy and the prayers that we offer for a beloved deceased are never static, magical moments, but are beginning points of a love process whereby we with Christ live the sacrifice of the cross in our daily life. To live the Liturgy is the best way of helping our beloved departed. It directs not only the love of Christ but also our own unique love, so desired still by our beloved departed, toward those who have gone on before us.

LOVE RETURNED

As our loved ones, living in the new life beyond this earth, receive continued love from Christ and from us who love in Christ's Spirit, they are progressively healed of their hurts and set free to love us with a new and more perfect love than that which they showed us while they were on earth.

Love begets love. The only true sign that our loved ones have been healed through the therapy of our love united with the love of the Saints and angels who love with the Spirit of Christ's love is their desire to return such love in loving service to others. And to whom would they turn to show such loving service if not to us to whom they are bonded by so many cords of intimate affection? They have a God-given loyalty toward us as a special gift whereby they now see us to have always been loyal toward them. With loving gratitude they stretch beyond the silent divide that seemingly separates them from us and in the mystery of loving presence they come to us.

How often I have felt united with my departed father! How often I have felt his loving intercession for me! Persons who have lost loved ones often have reported to me how present they are to their beloved ones. Would it be far fetched to believe that their love would go beyond the mere sentiment of love to enter into an actualization of that love by loving service to those still living on earth? Can anyone guarantee that when the departed are loved in Christ, they cannot return that love by sharing with us a protective hand in physical or psychological dangers that will prevent us from incurring great harm to ourselves? In our spiritual needs and our struggles with the forces of darkness around and within us, can our loved ones not respond with spiritual advice, better now than the advice they may have given us when they "sojourned" with us on earth?

We are dealing here with a mystery, one that cannot be described but only experienced by those who truly love others in Christ. The words of C.S. Lewis aptly summarize our meeting with our beloved departed in love and the possibility of communion with them: "It was quite incredibly unemotional. Just the impression of her *mind* momentarily facing my own. Mind, not 'soul' as we tend to think of soul. Certainly the reverse of what is called 'soulful.' Not at all like a rapturous reunion of lovers. Much more like getting a telephone call or a wire from her about some practical arrangement. Not that there was any 'message'—just intelligence and attention. No sense of joy or sorrow. No love even, in our ordinary sense. No un-love. I had never in any mood imagined the dead as being so—well, so business-like. Yet there was an extreme and cheerful intimacy. An intimacy that had not passed through the senses or the emotions at all."[4]

PRAYER TO A BELOVED DEPARTED

Dearest Beloved: I have such a strong desire to speak with you, to be present in love with you at this moment. You have left me and yet God has blessed me with your continued loving presence. Our love truly breaks through all man-conceived prison walls of what we can do through our loving union that spans all limitations placed on us by our physical separation from each other.

I seem to feel the need of going beyond the images and pictures I have of you. God assures me you live and you still can show that love which I need and so ardently desire from you. I feel now freed by the purifying grief and struggles endured after your death to turn to God and in Him I find you.

How real is this experience and yet how difficult it is to

share with others! In quiet moments I lift myself to God in total surrender and love. It is then that you become so very real to me. Again, it isn't a picture of you as I and the family always knew you. You are the ray and God is the sun. You come to me as light and I become a part of your light. And our lighted beings dance in brilliant splendor of God's light.

How humble I become in such flashing moments of union with you! I thank God that He incarnates His love for me in your love. And I praise Him that He has shown me that death need not be a part of sin, but can truly be unto God's glory and our continued growth in greater loving union with each other in Him.

I know you live! And I know we will never be separated from each other as long as we meet in and through the medium and the message of God's love for us, Jesus Christ. Your death has taught me that only death can free us to love each other in God. The words of St. John of the Cross daily take on more meaning in our oneness:

> I live, yet no true life I know,
>   and, living thus expectantly,
> I die because I do not die.

The more I die to my control over you, the more I live in your love. And the more real God becomes as I allow Him to bring us to new life in His love. My own death no longer holds any fear for me, for I know the real death is being undergone by you and me daily as we surrender ourselves to the great God, *the Consuming Fire* (Heb 12:29).

His life is our life. His eternal love is shared and experienced in our true love for each other. O, Divine Fire, burn and transform our love for each other into brilliant light and heat that drive out all ignorance and coldness of self-centeredness from both of us so that all barriers will truly fall and we will discover each other in Him who is all in all. Then we will know as for the first time that God is love and "there is only Christ: He is everything and he is in everything" (Col 3:11).

Footnotes

1. For the writings of such theologians see: Karl Rahner, *On the Theology of Death* (N.Y.: Herder & Herder, 1964), p. 42; Andre-Marie Dubarle, *The Biblical Concept of Original Sin* (N.Y.: Herder & Herder, 1964), pp. 235-237; Roger Troisfontaines, *I Do Not Die* (N.Y.: Desclée, 1963), pp. 194-195; L.L. Morris, "Death," in *New Bible Dictionary* (Grand Rapids, MI: Eerdmans, 1962), p. 301; William J. Rewak, "Adam, Immortality and Human Death," in *Sciences Ecclesiastiques*, 19 (1967), pp. 67-79.
2. C.S. Lewis, *A Grief Observed* (N.Y.: A Bantam Book-Seabury Press, Inc., 1961), p. 54.
3. K. Rahner, op. cit., pp. 21-39.
4. C.S. Lewis, op. cit., pp. 85-86.

CHAPTER TWO

MY GOD, I'M DYING

There is one day or night when you and I will find ourselves preparing to take that last breath. With that breath exhaled as a sigh, a gasp, a scream of anger or of fear or whatever be the circumstances some cord will be cut. We will begin our journey out of the womb of our earthly body and we will be launched into a new existence. What new horizons will open up to us? Will it be similar to what happened on the day of our physical birth from our mother's womb?

The details of our dying escape our power to control. Will we die in a hospital room? Will our loved ones gather around us and comfort us with their assuring love? Will we have the comfort of receiving the rites of the Church, especially the rite of reconciliation, the anointing of the sick and the Eucharist?

Will death come to us suddenly as a result of a heart attack or an accident on the highway or in a plane? Or will it be a lingering and crippling sickness that will allow us much time to be alone to ponder our inescapable fate?

Perhaps we have been putting the thought of our own death out of our mind for a good part of our life. But as we become older, more of our friends and acquaintances are dying. We find ourselves attending more and more wakes and funerals. We read the obituaries in our local daily newspaper just to be in touch with what is happening around us.

And the realization finally hits us one day. "My God, I, too, am going to die like all the rest of them!" In spite of the American myth in science's power to conquer nature, death must not be thought of for death attacks that naive myth only to laugh it out of reality. When we were younger, our work, our pursuit of success and the possession of more material possessions, absorption in travel, sports, recreation and sex could help us put off thinking of that last day of our earthly existence.

THIS IS IT!

But now, in this moment, we are nearing the end. Perhaps we have undergone the usual stages of resisting the reality of our death. We have gone through Dr. Kübler-Ross' various stages.[1] We had those first moments of shock at the news of the doctors that we were going to die. We denied it. They were wrong. They do make mistakes. They don't know what they are talking about. We vented our anger and resentment upon our loved ones who visited us, upon the professionals who were trying to help us, the nurses and doctors and other aids, and we treated them as our enemies. We knew in our head that some day we would die. But this could not be the time. We were not ready to pack our bags and go into the dark beyond.

There were so many unfulfilled plans. We had so much yet to accomplish in our life. Our family and friends needed us. How would they ever get along without our presence in their lives? We turned to God and began to bargain and set up conditions, things we would do to placate God's will so that He might extend our life a bit longer, for the time when we would be really ready to go. Then we were plagued over the weeks and months of pondering the possibility of our death, affirmed in so many ways, especially by our physical deterioration and general weakness. We could no longer function in many of the ways as we did before. We really were slipping, and fast, and this made us very depressed and filled us with sadness.

Finally we worked ourselves up to accept the inevitable. Everyone has to die some time. "Guess my time is now." The pains and sufferings are too much. Only a miracle would save us, we think, and God isn't listening to our plea for this to happen. Yes, death is around the corner! "God, I truly am dying and now!"

WHAT'S ON THE OTHER SIDE?

So now we really start pondering the great question that we have put off for so many years. As soon as the great cord is snapped that sends us flying through the planets and stars, through the heavens until we arrive at . . . yes, just where do we think we are going after we die? Our Christian faith and our study of the catechism have assured us that there is life after death. We believe there are such things as heaven, hell and purgatory that open their jaws to swallow all of us human beings, but only after we have been judged and sentenced to our just reward, for we were taught ". . . the amount you measure out is the amount you will be given back" (Lk 6:38).

We have always had faith in the fact that there is life after death. We were convinced of that fact in our childhood when faith was easy to come by. But as an adult it became perhaps a bit more difficult to believe since how can anyone prove such a fact until he gets there? And then one doesn't need faith any more. It is a real fact!

Such a reality, namely that we will live after we die, can be accepted only by faith. We cannot prove that reality as we can prove that two plus two make four. Is there a way to penetrate into the mystery of what awaits us after our death?

THE SCHOOL OF LOVE

In Dostoievsky's classical novel, *The Brothers Karamazov*, the author has a woman searching to rediscover her faith in a life after death in a dialogue with the famous holy monk, Father Zossima. She asks herself whether there really is any life beyond the grave or will there be just the thistles growing on her grave? Does she live only to disappear without a trace? She had faith as a child, but how can she as an adult have a faith in life after death? Where is she to look for proofs that will satisfy her reason and allay all her fears?

The holy Father Zossima gives her this answer:

> There's no proving it, though you can be convinced of it. . . . How? By the experience of active love. Strive to love your neighbor actively and indefatigably. In as far as you advance in love you will grow surer of the reality of God and of the immortality of your soul. If you attain to perfect self-forgetfulness in the love of your neighbor, then you will believe without doubt, and no doubt can possibly enter your soul. This has been tried. This is certain.[2]

Our life is made up of two curves. From the moment of our conception some 100 trillion cells have been on a journey of development which allows us to extend our presence as a *physical being*, an intellectual, loving person. That curve reaches a peak of physical development and after some twenty years the curve begins its gradual descent until the point of dissolution which we call death.

The other curve moves in an almost opposite direction. It is the development of our consciousness and growth on the level of *spiritual being* as an autonomous, self-positing free agent. Ideally, according to God's plan, this development not only should continue to reach new levels of unitive love between ourself and God, between ourself and other human beings but even the trials that accompany the break-down of our physical powers should be the occasions for our continued growth in love-consciousness.

THREE MOVEMENTS

God has created us to share in His eternal life. God is love (1 Jn 4:8) and if He loves each one of us, He wishes us to live as long as He does, and that is forever. Not only is love as strong as death, but love conquers death and transforms death itself into new levels of sharing in God's eternal life.

The first movement of our life as a sharing in God's life came when we were ushered into existence at the moment of our conception within the womb of our mother. We were called into existence. We were completely passive. Life was given to us. Evidently we had no choice for before we could make choices we had to exist.

The second movement in our life sends us to the end-moment of our earthly existence, namely, to our death. In a way, that moment is the most important moment of our entire earthly existence. That moment is the culmination and summation of all the moments of our life before the death moment. One could say we exist to reach this moment of death, as Jesus in His earthly existence lived for "His hour" of death.

That moment brings together and is conditioned by all previous choices. We are, at our death, the way we have chosen to live all through our life. It is the peak moment of consciousness and freedom in which we cast our fate for all eternity. This is the moment of choice to live in loving communion with God and neighbor, the way God wishes all human beings to live, in order to be happy and share in His life forever.

To choose to participate in a communion of love with God and neighbor is to experience God as love and ourselves as uniquely ourselves with a being that is immortal. Thus we do not so much reason to our life after death but we experience immortality as that quality of shared divine life in loving communion which our consciousness in the experience of loving union guarantees as love enduring forever.

The summary of the Christian life is found in experienced love of God and neighbor.

> We ourselves have known and put our faith in
> God's love towards ourselves.
> God is love
> and anyone who lives in love lives in God,
> and God lives in him.
> Love will come to its perfection in us
> when we can face the day of judgment without fear;
> because even in this world
> we have become as he is.
> In love there can be no fear,
> but fear is driven out by perfect love:
> because to fear is to expect punishment,
> and anyone who is afraid is still imperfect in love.
> We are to love, then,
> because he loved us first.
> Anyone who says, 'I love God,'
> and hates his brother,
> is a liar,
> since a man who does not love the brother that he can see
> cannot love God, whom he has never seen.
> So this is the commandment that he has given us,
> that anyone who loves God must also love his brother
>
> (1 Jn 4:16-21).

The third movement is found in the present *now* instant. This moment in which we find ourselves is a call from God to enter into a death-birth experience. It is God pouring His Spirit into the matrix of this human situation. It is the only place in which we begin to "pass over" from *non*-being to *true* being as consciously loving persons.

It is God offering us the awesome responsibility to choose life over death as we break away from the sin that keeps us imprisoned in our isolation, suffocating our true life by its stifling self-centeredness.

Jesus continually summoned His listeners to a decision to wake up from sleep and non-being. He calls us in this present moment, a moment that frees us from the past and opens us up to new life in a future which depends on our choice *now*. "So stay awake because you do not know either the day or the hour" (Mt 25:12).

The hour of our death is therefore not so unknown to us. Death is constantly present to us. As we choose life over death, over selfishness by living in loving service toward God and neighbor, we are determining both our death and our passage into eternal life even now.

BUT WHY MUST I DIE?

But the burning question as we picture ourselves in that final moment between earthly life and absolute death is: "Why must I die?" It is an urgent question that demands an answer. We have all seen death overcome and snuff out the life of our father or mother, wife or husband, a child or a dear friend. We have witnessed their struggle, pain and suffering.

Why must we die if the present moment alone is all important? Scripture gives us a somewhat vague, inconclusive answer. "For the wage paid by sin is death" (Rm 6:23). God in the Genesis story commanded man and woman not to eat of the fruit of the tree of life. "You must not eat it, nor touch it, under pain of death" (Gn 3:3). They sinned and God decreed: "For dust you are and to dust you shall return" (Gn 3:19).

WAGES OF SIN

Did sin bring us *physical* death? Would Adam and Eve have lived indefinitely, never tasting physical death had they not sinned? Is death, in these passages, to be understood as referring exclusively or even primarily to the physical cessation of human life as we have known it during our earthly existence? Or are there other aspects that sin has introduced to what would otherwise have been a natural passage through physical death to a higher evolutive level of human existence?

All around us are signs of a basic law of development, that death is an indispensable condition of biological evolution. Jesus not only clearly taught this but He lived out in His own life this dialectic of death that leads to higher development, to resurrection, to unity in love. He taught selfish isolation must be surrendered to communion if we are to enjoy eternal life.

> I tell you, most solemnly,
> unless a wheat grain falls on the ground and dies,
> it remains only a single grain;
> but if it dies,
> it yields a rich harvest.
> Anyone who loves his life loses it,
> anyone who hates his life in this world
> will keep it for the eternal life (Jn 12:24-25).

There is no way, in the teaching of Jesus, for His disciples to have a part with Him except through the denial of a lower level of self-possession. He called them to follow *Him*, and the condition He laid down was the repudiation of their false self to take up a cross each day and, under obedience to His commandments, to love others as He had first loved them. "If anyone wants to be a follower of mine, let him renounce himself and take up his cross every day and follow me. For anyone who wants to save his life will lose it; but anyone who loses his life for my sake, that man will save it" (Lk 9:23-24; Mt 16:24-27; Mk 8:34-38).

He was the Divine Seed that fell into the earth only to die and rise to new life that He might share that new life with us human beings created by the Father according to the Son's image (Gn 1:26). How beautifully the poet, Francis Thompson, captured this universal law of greater growth in human development in his *Ode to the Setting Sun*:

> For there is nothing lives but something dies,
> And there is nothing dies but something lives.
>   Till skies be fugitives,
> Till Time, the hidden root of change, updries,
> Are Birth and Death inseparable on earth;
>   For they are twain yet one, and Death is Birth.[3]

But if death is so positive, why do you and I fear our physical death so much? Does not sin add something to what might have been a very natural progression to a higher development of human existence? Many of the early Church Fathers, as well as Scripture itself and an adequate understanding of various Church councils down through the ages, lead us to a proper understanding of just what sin does add to death. In other words, it is not against our Christian faith that God could have taken us all up into a new life through a transformation that we call death even if mankind had never sinned.

The Greek Fathers call the death of Mary, the Mother of God, her dormition. She died physically but because of her sinlessness her death did not cause her any fear of a possible separation from God as her source of life. Rather her death was her transformation into glory. In the Byzantine Matins the *Irmos* reads:

In thee, O spotless Maid,
The bounds of nature are overstepped:
Childbearing is virginal.
Death is but a pledge of life.
After giving birth thou art a maiden.
After death alive.
O Godbearer,
Thou dost save us, thy heritage,
Unceasingly![4]

DEATH AS AN UPHEAVAL AND SEPARATION

We might believe through deep faith that life follows death. But on a very gut-level we harbor fears, just as Jesus did as He faced the prospect of His demise. He truly believed and expected joyfully that He would be raised to new life after His death, but, in the throes of agony in the Garden of Gethsemani and hanging on the cross breathing His last breath, Jesus cried out in terrifying fear at the seeming abandonment of His Heavenly Father. He really prayed in the Garden that the Father would remove from Him the cup of death. He shook with fear and sweated drops of blood.

So on our death-bed we, too, will probably experience fear and agony. Death does not happen merely to our "body" and not to our soul. The whole person will die. You will die as I will die. And that is a radical suffering, an upheaval of tremendous order. As it affects our whole person, we will be consciously dying. On one level we will experience death passively. It happens to us as it happens to all human beings. No one escapes dying. In this sense we are all equal. Death is no respecter of persons. We cannot buy any withholding of death's sentence upon our earthly existence. It will most surely happen to you and me. On another level, we will experience death actively to the extent that we consciously accept death in loving surrender to the Father's will as Jesus did. "Not my will but thine be done" (Lk 22:42).

It is usually the separation element that brings to us so much fear and anxiety about death. Death always comes too definitively, sparing no one. It always comes to us all too soon. We have so many more things to do. What will our loved ones do without us? Our body gradually becomes a worn out organism, bringing with its dissolution a lot of pain and suffering.

If God is so loving, how can He permit or even send us such suffering and pain? Why so much horrendous tearing apart in the separation of ourselves from this lower existence to one of higher consciousness?

That is precisely what Scripture would call the "wage of sin" in death. Is it only God who "punishes" us through our sins by such sufferings? Or is it because, as St. Paul claims and we admit, there is sin in our members (Rm 7:23)? Our false ego holds on to control life so that we can, so we think, live independently of God, "free" of surrendering in trust to God and in loving service to neighbor. We bring so much of our own suffering and pain upon ourselves because we fear and do not live in child-like abandonment to God's infinite love for us. We need to enter into a sense of being estranged from our true self, of entering into battle with the demonic powers within us, of feeling, as Jesus did on the cross, as though we are abandoned by God Himself in order that we can truly scream as He did to see the face of the Father. The Spanish philosopher, Ortega y Gasset writes: "All the rest is rhetoric, posturing, farce. He, who does not really feel himself lost, is without remission; that is to say, he never finds himself, never comes up against his own reality." [5]

THE SWEETNESS OF DEATH

Unfortunately much of the popular writing about near-death experience tends to gloss over the existential suffering involved in this rending experience of death. Dr. Kübler-Ross, Dr. R.A. Moody, Dr. Karlis Osis and many other reputable scientists have published the results of their research into actual cases of persons who entered into the death-experience and came out of it to return to life to report a most pleasant experience that took away any fear of death.[6]

Regardless, as in the case of Jesus, how sanctified we may become by God's grace, there will always be a passivity mingled to the physical and psychic sufferings that frequently accompany death. There is a definitive end to our "natural" way of existing through a material body in space and time relationships to the rest of the material world around us. We have known no other form of existence, except the limitations of life in the womb.

But there is a more essential element involved in death that is linked to higher transformation into communion through love that can carry us through death's agonies by faith, hope and love, gifts of God. As we have lived daily in our choices as a bodied being, we have become a *person*, the unique person God wants us to be as we freely have given ourselves in love to God and neighbor.

What happens to us individually on the biological level of physical dissolution, a dissolution that can often be accompanied by tremendous sufferings and pains, is commonly shared with all human beings. It's much like birth. In our coming forth from our mother's womb we passively "suffered" that common pain which brought us to an expanded horizon of human development. So, too, in death. We can do very little but "suffer" death to happen to us.

But about the "act" of receiving our death and cooperating as we choose to meet God and our neighbor in love in that moment, the climax of so many other moments throughout our life to live in communion and not selfish isolation, we can do very much. We can freely, as Jesus did in the agony in the Garden of Gethsemani and on the cross, order this act toward our ultimate end, God. Karl Rahner well expresses this aspect of death, our active cooperation which leads to transformation:

> But how man dies his death and how he understands it, depends on the decision of his freedom. Here he does not carry something imposed on him, but what he chooses himself. That is to say: in the deed of the dying existence, man is necessarily free in his attitude toward death. Although he has to die, he is asked how he wishes to do it. For, existence conscious of itself must unavoidably see the end. It sees this end all through life, perhaps dimly and not explicitly. It may happen that it will purposely avoid looking at it, or it will simply overlook it (but still will realize it all the same). Inasmuch as man freely takes upon himself this existence tending toward the end, he also freely accepts the movement toward the end.[7]

SUFFERING UNTO GLORY

We will never be able to understand logically the mystery of suffering and pain, not only that which accompanies our dying moments, but also that which enters into so much of our earthly existence. We can argue that the sufferings which prepare us for death can become a blessed occasion when they help us to realize our helplessness in the face of death. Single-handed we are powerless in our battle with imminent death. Our pride and spirit of independence can be broken by the humiliations of our sufferings that often cause us to seek the help of so many persons around us for the most ordinary things of life which we were always able to handle by ourselves before.

As Job found out, suffering will always remain a mystery to our puny reasoning powers. But the Christian understands through the infusion of the Holy Spirit that there is an inward dimension to suffering and death, an element that is immortal and incorruptible which places the Christian beyond the ravages of decay and pain. That inward dimension lies in God and the indwelling trinitarian life that unfolds within all human beings, giving us the power to bring life where there are seemingly only suffering and death.

God sent His Son into our world to reconcile us to Himself (Col 1:20). Jesus Christ came not to tell us the answer to the universal problem of evil, but to overcome evil, sin and death by His suffering love. Division and dissension, hatred and fear, aggressive power and exploitation could be conquered only by a gentle, suffering love unto death. By freely sacrificing His human life in dying for us, Jesus in His humanity was raised to glory by His Father's Spirit and is now able to live within us.

"Was it not ordained that the Christ should suffer and so enter into his glory?" (Lk 24:25-26). Jesus' answer to evil in the world is suffering love. He came with none of Caesar's power. His power would be in His weakness and emptiness: "For God's foolishness is wiser than human wisdom, and God's weakness is stronger than human strength" (1 Cor 1:25).

The depths of Jesus' suffering, especially on the cross as He suffers and dies, not as a victim of circumstances but as one who freely accepts His sufferings and death as a part of His Father's will, can be understood only in terms of the infinite love He received in His human consciousness from His heavenly Father. Love begets love as life begets life.

St. Paul constantly realized that Jesus, the Son of God, sacrificed Himself for his sake (Gal 2:20). This suffering servant, Jesus, is always loving each one of us personally unto death. He lives within us and has that same, consuming love for us as He had on the cross. We, too, in the sufferings that we bear in our earthly pilgrimage, especially in our moments before death, can say with St. Paul: "I have been crucified with Christ, and I live now not with my own life but with the life of Christ who lives in me. The life I now live in this body I live in faith; faith in the Son of God who loved me and who sacrificed himself for my sake" (Gal 2:20-21).

THE SPIRIT GIVES US A NEW HEART

The pierced heart of Jesus on the cross (Jn 19:34) proves to us His love unto death. Jesus, passing through death, is glorified and can pour out His Spirit (Jn 7:39) upon us and upon all mankind. The Spirit is life-giving, driving out all the fears that suffering and death may bring us by pouring God's perfect love into our hearts (1 Jn 4:18; Rm 5:5). With a new "heart" or consciousness through the outpouring of deeper faith, hope and love of the Spirit, we, too, will be empowered to bear all things out of love of God and neighbor. Then in our preparation for death we will grasp what no human mind can attain by mere human reasoning: that death, when it drags us painfully through the purification of suffering, is the portal through which we pass in a transformation unto glory.

> If we have died with him, then we shall live with him.
> If we hold firm, then we shall reign with him (2 Tm 2:11).

PRAYER ON MY DEATH-BED

"From the depths I call to you, Yahweh,
Lord, listen to my cry for help!
Listen compassionately
    to my pleading!
If you never overlooked our sins, Yahweh,

Lord, could anyone survive?
But you do forgive us:
   and for that we revere you.

I wait for Yahweh, my soul waits for him,
   I rely on his promise,
   my soul relies on the Lord
   more than a watchman on the coming of dawn" (Ps 130:1-6).

God, You seem so far away!
I need You as I never have needed You before.
I seem to be covered with darkness.
And I am so cold and lonely.

Friends come and visit;
and then I am again alone.
I have never felt so alone in my whole life.
Pain runs through my wasted body;
but it is nothing compared to the gnawing pain
   I feel in my heart.

My brain seems so confused.
I cannot pray; only distractions
and crazy ideas come to me
whenever I think of You.

I know I am dying, God.
My strength is slipping away
   and I am so tired.
I almost want death to come;
and, yet, I am afraid, Lord!
What's on the other side, God?
Now I see only darkness.

Will You really be waiting
   to catch me when I make the leap?
Will I just die like an animal
   and go back to dust?
Or is there really life, eternal life
ahead for me, over that threshold

where Death is the ticket-taker?

Will the movie be a good one, Lord?
A double feature?
A comedy or maybe a tragedy?

God, I really want to believe
that You love me and are waiting for me.
I believe, I believe, I believe!

But what more can I do?
Father, into Your hands I commend my spirit.
Have mercy on me, a sinner!

Come, Lord Jesus, and lead me
    home to our Father.
I need You, Jesus.
I trust You as my Lord and Savior.
I love You and abandon myself
    into Your guiding light.
Lead, kindly Light.
I surrender to You,
MY HOPE AND MY SALVATION!

Footnotes

1. Dr. E. Kübler-Ross, *On Death and Dying* (N.Y.: Macmillan Company, 1969) pp. 34 ff.
2. Fyodor Dostoievsky, *The Brothers Karamazov*, tr. from the Russian by Constance Garnett (N.Y.: Modern Library, Random House, n.d.), p. 55.
3. Francis Thompson, "Ode to the Setting Sun" in *Victorian and Later Poets*, editors: J. Stephens, E. Beck, Royal Snow (N.Y.: American Book Company, 1967) p. 1081.
4. Translated by John Ryder, S.J., *Eastern Rite Prayers to the Mother of God* (N.Y.: Russian Center, Fordham Univ., 1955), p. 42.
5. Jose Ortega y Gasset, *The Revolt of the Masses* (N.Y.: W.W. Norton & Co., 1932) p. 157.

6. Cf. E. Kübler-Ross, *On Death and Dying* (N.Y.: Macmillan Company, 1969); *Questions and Answers on Death and Dying* (N.Y.: Macmillan Company, 1974); *Death: The Final Stage of Growth* (Englewood Cliffs, N.J.: Prentice-Hall, Inc., 1975); R.A. Moody: *Life After Life* (Atlanta: Mockingbird Books, 1977); Dr. Karlis Osis and Dr. Erlendur Haraldsson: *What They Saw . . . At the Hour of Death* (N.Y.: Avon Books, 1977).

7. Karl Rahner, *On the Theology of Death* (N.Y.: Herder & Herder, 1961), tr. Charles H. Henkey.

CHAPTER THREE

PURGATORY: THERAPY OF LOVE

To the degree that we love others and also receive from them their unselfish love for us, so will we believe in immortal life, life that is a sharing in God's unending love. For God has created us to share in this love. If His love is infinite, our yearning for such communion in love will also be unending, knowing no moment of complete fulfillment or static rest.

We must often ask ourselves, "After I die, what sort of eternal life awaits me on the other side?" God's revelation assures us, as we have already seen, that, dying physically, we do pass into a new form of existence that will be eternal life. What quality of life, we wonder, is there in that eternal kingdom?

In the past two decades we have seen much literature that describes the experiences of persons who have had a near-death experience and returned to tell us what kind of life awaited them on the "other side."[1] Dr. R.A. Moody, in his famous bestseller, *Life After Life*,[2] has done much to popularize such experiences of people who have in many cases been pronounced "clinically dead" but who have returned to life to describe in vivid detail the type of experiences they had as they passed over to the other side.

Death is described as a transition into a new life that generally brings great peace and joy to the one undergoing the experience. Usually there is the sensation of a journey down a long corridor that opens up to beautiful light and the appearance of familiar relatives and friends who welcome them into the new life. Transcendence is a common characteristic of such experiences as the persons are lifted up into a foreign region or new dimension of great light and beauty. Sometimes there is a series of autoscopic experiences with a self-visualization from a position of height that allows the "dead" person to travel through space by means of some "etheric" or "astral" body. When they return to their physical bodies they usually bring with them a new perspective which drives away any fear of dying.

Let us not delay here on this subject, for is there not a danger of building an optimism that will not be a true statement of the life that is beyond death from the subjective, psychological descriptions of such reports? Faith, through Scripture and the guiding teaching of the Church, assures us that we will not only live after death but that we will be the same person, recognizable by those others who have also passed beyond this earth. We will be capable of entering into communication with them. We will have the same level of consciousness attained while we were developing ourselves on earth. This will mean that, just as here we have memories of experiences with friends, so also we will remember and love the same friends with at least the same degree of unselfish love reached through our relationships with them on earth.

But as on earth, so beyond earthly existence, we will long for continued growth in our relationships with our friends whom we love. St. Paul warns us not to be concerned with what he calls "stupid" questions (1 Cor 15:36), such as what kind of a body we will have in the future life. He assures us that what is sown will be harvested in a more beautiful, enriching manner than anything we could expect. But, in order to guide us to make choices through the freeing power of love as exercised now which will be a part of preparing ourselves to be what we will be like in the future, it is good to follow the teaching of the Church on one of the states that awaits us after death, namely, *Purgatory*. This teaching of an intermediate state after death has not always been well presented by Church teachers through the centuries and, therefore, has not always been well understood by the faithful in its importance and essence.

A PLACE OF PUNISHMENT

In the West St. Augustine developed a very concrete doctrine of Purgatory, based on his interpretation of 1 Cor 3:11-16. From his teaching we have been given the notion of a place to which those not yet purified must go to be purified by a cleansing fire in order to expiate for the temporal punishment due to forgiven mortal sins and for venial sins not explicitly forgiven.[3] The legalistic accent was stressed and did not take into serious consideration the laws of growth and development of human personhood.

A STATE OF HEALING

In the East, the existence of purgatory and the accent on making "satisfaction" through temporal punishments by fire were never well-defined or separated from the teaching of Hell. Drawing from Holy Scripture, patristic homilies, liturgical services, the lives of the Saints and certain revelations and visions of life after death, the Eastern writers describe a state of healing therapy, brought about by the prayers of the Church and individuals still living on earth, especially as presented in the context of the Divine Liturgy.

New teaching in the West begins, not from a separation of a physical body from a compartmentalized soul, but from the awareness that we are "whole" persons who will continue to exist after death with the same personality. Hence we will have the same relationships on a social level with those persons who have "formed" us for better or for worse into the unique human beings that we are.[4] Our development as a human being, made according to God's own image and likeness (Gn 1:26), can never be brought to a statically fixed point. If there is any punishment that awaits us, it will come, not so much from God's vindictive spirit or His sense of strict reprisal, but rather from God's justice working through His everlasting, merciful love to help us see the incongruity and lack of harmony in our earthly living and to bring us healing as we painfully strive to become our *true* self.

Psychologists claim that most of us earthlings develop only about four and a half to five percent of our psychic powers. Do we not often feel that there is so much more capability within us than we are realizing? Why should we expect that God would limit the giving of Himself to us in love, and this in a consciously developed personal relationship, to merely this earthly existence? Do we think perhaps that God only operates according to our experience of time and, therefore, that He ceases to operate in our regard after we die?

Death frees us from the very narrow perspective that sin and death have given to us and opens us up to cosmic dimensions of communication between ourselves and all of God's creation. The inherited limitations of our own genetic pre-programming along with our own willful decisions to act in opposition to God's Spirit of love, to say nothing of the negative influences which others who have entered into our earthly sojourn have left upon us are all brought with us as intrinsic parts of our personality.

Karl Rahner likens Purgatory to a "full ripening" of the whole person after death:

The many dimensions of men do not all attain their perfection simultaneously and hence there is a full ripening of the whole man "after death," as his basic decision penetrates the whole extent of this reality. In this concept . . . the remission of punishment [is not] a mere abstention from punishing but rather . . . the process of painful integration of the whole of man's stratified being into the definitive decision about his life, taken under the grace of God. . . . We cannot indeed picture to ourselves how in particular such a process of maturing can develop in different ways in the life after death; but *that* such a thing is conceivable will be very difficult to dispute a priori.[5]

HEALING LOVE

God is love and God is "Raphael" (Ex 15:27), the one who heals. Christianity's uniqueness is its accent on *incarnationalism*. God loves His material world. He communicates to us and is in *communion* with us. God's love is developed, revealed and made perfect as we love one another unselfishly (1 Jn 4:12).

Church is the concentration of God's self-giving in love through the sacrifice of His Son, Jesus Christ, given to and shared by human beings who reveal God's infinite love in a transformed, new creation through the Spirit of the risen Lord. And Church never ends for it moves from glory to glory (2 Cor 3:18) into the likeness of Christ. When will we human beings ever become perfect as our Heavenly Father is perfect (Mt 5:48)? When will we, "knowing the love of Christ, which is beyond all knowledge, be filled with the utter fullness of God" (Ep 3:19)?

Each one of us individually, and the corporate Body of Christ collectively (of which we are living members), will never know a moment in eternity when our love of God and neighbor will stop growing. At least we will always be open to the possibility of such growth.

Yet we see that our greatest growth in this life consists in the widening of our perspectives as we live in participated, loving communion with more and more persons. God's laws of progressive development of consciousness, through love in growing unity as well as our own unique diversity from others in this unity, operate in God's eternal *now* that can know no end. God's mercy is above all His works.

And we surely will be able to meet God immediately and directly as well as in His creatures, especially in other human beings. We will experience His healing love in life after death as we have encountered His healing love in this life. If we have received His healing love in this life through the concern of loved ones here, why should God stop healing us of our pains, hurts and fears through our loved ones and the many other beautiful, God-filled human beings we now call Saints in the life after our death?

HELPED BY OTHERS

The basic conviction of Christianity is that God makes use of other human beings to gift us with Himself. He consents in our history of salvation to give Himself to us in matter, in the humanity of His Son. He "needed" or consented to cooperate with free-will decisions of individuals like Abraham, Moses, David, Mary and Joseph, the Apostles, other Christians and non-Christians, to transform us into His children and co-heirs of Heaven with Christ (Rm 8:17).

The Church has always taught us to pray for each other. We share by Baptism the priesthood of the one High Priest, Jesus Christ, "It follows, then, that his power to save is utterly certain, since he is living for ever to intercede for all who come to God through him" (Heb 7:25).

God's healing love will continue to come to us after our death through the powerful intercession of Christ, localized and made incarnate for us, made accessible and capable of being experienced by us, through the love of our loved ones still on this earth. This is expressed most surely in the Church's constant encouragement to those still left on earth to pray and thus help the departed ones in Purgatory. Prayer and sacrifice offered in love bring healing to those in need of therapy in the life to come. It is God's love coming to us in the love we have for one another when we love as Christ loves us, with Christ loving within us.

> We ourselves have known and put faith in
> God's love towards ourselves.
> God is love
> and anyone who lives in love lives in God,
> and God lives in him (1 Jn 4:16).

Have you ever worked with a neurotic person? That person has built up, through fears and guilt, a false ego, an unreal world in which he or she dwells behind barriers and defenses, role playing and masks assumed. Such a person is incapable of self-healing. It is only love, unselfishly given from outside, that can drive away such fears and break down the unreal constructs that exist only in the perception of the fearful, neurotic person. It is perfect love that casts out all fear (1 Jn 4:18).

In a similar way after our death we will have certain areas of our life that we have constructed. Many relationships between ourselves and our friends, acquaintances and so-called "enemies" have evolved to fill us still with smouldering, inner volcanoes of hatred, anger, fear, dread, worry, confusion, tension and guilt. We reach out in our loneliness and self-centeredness, like a person in prison stretches through barred windows to contact help outside, to be "birthed" into new levels of being our true selves. As in this life, so in the life to come, we will recognize all too painfully that such healing love can come only from persons who freely and unselfishly love us in our true self in Christ. He is God's image according to whom we have been called into being and in whom alone we find our true uniqueness by knowing our place in His Body. This is the transformed segment of God's creation that has been "re-capitulated" by Christ's Spirit of love back to the Father unto His glory.

While we were on earth we knew how the love of our dear ones brought us into a new-founded state of self-identity. We literally felt a resurrection from the dead as we left the darkness of isolation and loneliness and entered into the light of warm love by their guiding hands of love for us. The healing power of love consists in the therapy of destroying isolation and building a community, a oneness, a togetherness in loving union.

PRAYERS AS LOVE

But how, we ask, can these whom we leave behind on earth when we die love us in such a way that we will be helped and can actually grow from darkness into light, from a level of confinement to one of freedom as we experience a new growth in love? We do not need "things," material gifts of flowers, rings, candy or clothing from them to express to us their love. Nor can love be merely expressed in words. I am sure after death you and I will be given an ability to pierce through so much of the gestures and language, that we on earth once called "sophistication," to get right into the inner heart and motivation of our loved ones. We will be able to "read" their hearts and we will know with the inerrancy of children who can know when they are being truly loved by parents and others that our friends are truly sending to us their unselfish love.

We will not be deceived. We will "know that we know that we know" who of our beloved friends continue to love and miss us. We will "see" how they miss us by their constant crying out to communicate with us. They will not be content only with placing a flower on our grave or having Masses said by some priest, but they will live out those symbols of flowers and the sacrifice and sacrament of love of Jesus as they live and pray for us in a consciously loving way.

True love means expressing in words and symbols: "I live my life for you, so that you will always be happy, so that you may live for ever and never know anything but new enriching growth." Death may change the nature of our relating to the loved ones whom we leave behind but the bond of love that ties us to them still remains and this love can become even stronger as it becomes purer than it was before. All too often in this earthly existence we say we love others, but our grief when they depart can show us, if we reflect honestly before God, that we miss them more for what they brought into our lives than for the privilege it was to lovingly serve them unto their sole happiness. Such idols need to be broken. The faith-dimension allows for continued and even stronger communication after death. But that is perhaps why so many of us will suffer. And the symbol used in religious writings to describe this suffering is Purgatory, a state of pain like a burning, searing fire. Friends no longer come to us in their physical presence and they settle for grieving. But their grief is often their own self-centered regret that they have lost us. We are no longer present to them to "help" them as they wish to be helped.

OFFERING THE EUCHARIST

The Church constantly tells us that the most perfect expression of love on the part of those still on earth toward one who has departed is to offer not only prayers but *the* most perfect prayer of Jesus Christ to His Father on our behalf, the Eucharist. The Divine Liturgy, as offered by Catholics, Orthodox and Anglicans, is the enactment in our human time of the eternal *now* (the *kairos*) sacrifice of Jesus Christ on behalf of the living and the dead, all who have been created in the triune love to be one in His Body.

Jesus Christ died once and for all on behalf of each human being (cf. Heb 9:28). His intercessory power is perfect and unlimited. "He is always able to save those who approach God through Him, since He forever lives to make intercession for them" (Heb 7:25). And His intercession knows no division or separation between those on earth, in Purgatory or in Heaven. The Church in its liturgical "re-presentation" of His sacrifice is the "place" where all human beings can meet in His almighty love, have their loves purified and be themselves empowered to love one another with His divine-human love. Christ is the Lamb of God who takes away our sins and heals the brokenness of all. But He brings that healing love to those in need through His Church, His Body which extends Himself to all in this life and in the life to come.

To offer the Liturgy for us in Purgatory, our friends need to enter by faith into the eternal life of the triune God, but specifically, through the life of the historical Christ in His incarnation, death and resurrection. Both those who offer this sacrifice of Christ and we for whom it is offered enter into a oneness with Christ through His Spirit. Our friends offer prayers for us in the Divine Liturgy, uniting their love with Christ's infinite love for us. It is not a magical rite made up of incantations or sterile gestures that are non-involving of the hearts of those who offer them with the heart of Christ. What releases healing love into our heart, crying out for new life, is when our loved ones "consociate" with Christ by putting on His mind. "Your mind must be renewed by a spiritual revolution so that you can put on the new self that has been created in God's way, in the goodness and holiness of the truth" (Ep 4:23-24).

Offering the sacrifice of Christ in the context of the Church's offering of the Divine Liturgy on our behalf necessitates that our loved ones see it as a beginning point, to be enfleshed by their dying to selfishness in their regard to us and by their rising to a sharing in the resurrection of Christ as they strive to bring us into complete happiness and immortal life. What heals us through their prayers and almsgiving and other sacrifices offered up by them for us is that such actions are a part of their living the eucharistic sacrifice of unselfish love. It is this sacrament of love as ongoing that brings about the healing of our brokenness through the therapy of love which we experience in Purgatory. Now we can see that Purgatory is not a static place of physical fire and punishing pain but a localization of loved ones centered in Christ in their love for us, living to call us into new levels of being.

BITTERSWEET

We can see in the doctrine of Purgatory that true love is the medium of communicating between the living and the dead. Love alone brings about "presence," as Blessed Robert Southwell, S.J., the 16th century English martyr, beautifully expressed it in a poem already quoted: "Not where I breathe do I live, but where I love." In Purgatory we will experience joy and pain as two sides of the same coin. We cannot really enter into a higher union with God, our neighbor and the entire cosmos unless we are ready to suffer the rending of our former possessive views of reality. And such a rending is always painful and agonizing. How we fear to let go of lower levels of what we have convinced ourselves is true security and a vital part of what makes us who we are! How much more we fear to stretch forward over the abyss of what seems to be nothing but darkness and let go of the confining possessiveness that is our present state of being!

How beautifully the bittersweet state of Purgatory is expressed by St. Catherine of Genoa:

> I believe no happiness can be found worthy to be compared with that of a soul in Purgatory except that of the saints in Paradise; and day by day this happiness grows as God flows into these souls, more and more as the hindrance to his entrance is consumed. Sin's rust is the hindrance, and the fire burns the rust away so that more and more the soul opens itself up to the divine inflowing. . . . As the rust lessens and the soul is opened up to the divine ray, happiness grows; until the time be accomplished the one wanes and the other waxes. . . . As for the will: never can the souls say these pains are pains, so contented are they with God's ordaining with which, in pure charity, their will is united.[6]

PURGATORY IS REAL

Purgatory is real, as real as love is. It is as necessary to us in the life to come as the cross or dying to selfishness is to us now in our earthly existence. There can be no new happiness, no deeper experience of union with God and our neighbor except through the healing that love of God and loving friends bring us. As we readily accept this love for us now and let go of our brokenness in the healing power of such love, so upon death this process of healing continues.

How consoling and grateful we should be to accept from the Church's teaching, not explicitly found in Scripture,[7] but constantly proclaimed by the Church, that we can grow in our life to come. This ancient teaching springs out of the social "connectedness" that love binds us all in Christ's Body, the Church, and is unto healing and growth in new levels of love-perfection. If one member of the Body suffers, the healthy members come to the aid of the weak (1 Cor 12:26).

Departing into life eternal and leaving behind our beloved

ones, we not only can be in contact through loving prayer in Christ, but such communication can be constant and of a higher nature than what we enjoyed with our loved ones on earth. The life of God in us knows no end of growth. Purgatory is a vital part of Heaven. Suffering and pain accepted in love can be unto glory through the healing of love given us by those who still remember us with a love that is the very love of Christ in us and them, bringing all of us into greater oneness of a life that will always open up to greater life.

PRAYER OF A DEPARTED PERSON
TO A LOVED ONE HERE ON EARTH

Dearest Beloved! Before that day when you held my hand for the last time and kissed me goodbye, how many beautiful times we shared together. How can I ever thank you for the gift of yourself to me! How many times I experienced the "passover" experience in those moments when you led me out of my fear and ignorance, from the darkness into the light of new being in a fresh oneness with you.

But then that last day came. I was split into two parts as I saw your tears telling me you didn't want me to leave you, that you would miss me as I would miss you. How to stay with you and yet how to push on to where God's Spirit of love was leading me? You saw the confusion written on my face as I confessed my ignorance of how to do both.

Yet it happened. Something split open and I was flying through spaceless space. Stars, planets, aeons of time, periods in the creation of this universe flashed before me. I stretched out and found I was myself, but now existing in a new and wonderful way of relating to reality. Things and persons, even you, were not less real and present to me, but I felt now I was knowing them, no longer darkly, as in a mirror, but somehow in a new "face to face" oneness (1 Cor 13:12).

How can I tell you the same applies to you, Beloved? You are not less present to me now than before on earth but much more so. Remember how I used to wait for your phone call or a letter when distance separated us? Now I am constantly in communication with you. I send you my love and pray for you to enter into something of my happiness.

But there is pain, too. I grieve to remember how I failed to have loved you unselfishly and so many others God sent into my life. My whole being reaches out to tell you and them of my sorrow. I see so much selfishness in me. My fears haunt me like nightmares. Black bats of forgotten refusals to love beat my face like swimmers, thrown by stormy waves on shredding rocks.

How to escape such a confining loneliness? The pain of wanting God with feverish thirst and to embrace you and all the world of His creation with love, but to be held in this tight-vice of squeezing selfishness—what agony! The evil in my heart and the tremendous tightness in my throat forces me to my knees.

And then, I feel a loosening. The burning fire cools as I feel your loving presence come over me. I know it is at such moments that you are loving me. You are telling me that you are willing to do anything for me that I might be eternally happy. What precious moments of healing love! Your prayers and sacrifices release me from my lack of love. Your love expressed for me indeed makes God's love to be experienced anew.

Please live in that love. And know my love for you needs expression toward you, too. As I am brought out of darkness and live in God's light, I am able to be more present and loving to you. Love truly begets love. Sufferings now endured bring me closer to you, to God, and to the whole of God's creation. O bittersweet passage through death to life through the purifying cross! Absence brings presence. Darkness is driven out by light. Love alone remains forever!

Footnotes

1. Some of the writings on a scientific level or very popular level that have dealt with this problem are: E. Kübler-Ross, *On Death and Dying*, op. cit.; R.A. Moody, op. cit.; Dr. Karlis Osis and Dr. Erlendur Haraldsson, op. cit; Anne Sandberg, *Seeing the Invisible* (Plainfield, N.J.: Logos International, 1977); Elizabeth Bossert, *My Visit to Heaven* (Jacksonville, FL: Higley, 1968); Gordon Lindsay, *Paradise, Abode of the Righteous-Dead* (Dallas: The Voice of Healing, 1967); Karl Sabiers, *Where Are the DEAD?* (Los Angeles: Christian Pocket Bks., 1959); Anne Terry White, *All About the Stars* (N.Y.: Random House, 1954).
2. *Life After Life* (Atlanta, Ga.: Mockingbird Bks., 1975).
3. Cf. F. Cayre, *Manual of Patrology* (Tournai: Desclée & Co., 1936), Vol. 1, p. 712.
4. Representative of such new thinking about Purgatory is Karl Rahner in his work: *On the Theology of Death*, op. cit.
5. *Ibid.*, pp. 347-354.
6. St. Catherine of Genoa, *On Purgatory*, tr. Charlotte Balfour and Helen D. Irvine (N.Y.: Sheed & Ward, 1946), pp. 18-19.
7. Chief among the texts found in Scripture and referred to by the teaching Church are 2 M 12:45-46 and 1 Cor 3:13-15. These texts would only support the doctrine that gradually developed from the early Church's universal practice of offering prayers, alms and the Divine Liturgy on behalf of the departed.

CHAPTER FOUR

THE COMMUNION OF SAINTS

If we have just lost a loved one, we nonetheless believe him or her to be fully alive in the new life given to those who depart the confines of this world. All the relationships, conscious thoughts and loving desires our loved ones had before death are still very much with them and even cry out for greater fulfillment.

But have we given enough consideration to actually putting that belief into practice by asking them to assist us who, in their love for us, can and really do ardently wish to help us through their active love for us? If they are alive in their new life and still can communicate with us, depending on the intensity of their love for us and our love for them, ought we not believe their love prompts them to help us in whatever ways they can in order that we might come to share in their happiness?

TEACHING OF THE CHURCH

We do not need merely to "hope" that we can make contact in love with our loved ones. It is a firmly established tradition in Christian teaching that all Christians form one Body of Christ. "There is one Body, one Spirit, just as you were all called into one and the same hope when you were called.

There is one Lord, one faith, one baptism, and one God who is Father of all, over all, through all and within all" (Ep 4:4-6). Christ, through His death and resurrection, has been constituted by His Father the Head of this Body.

This Body knows no separation between the members and the Head and among the numbers who are still on earth or are now in Heaven or Purgatory, among the members of the Church militant, triumphant or suffering.[1] This fellowship in Christ links all Christians together under Christ by the bonds of faith, the sacraments, especially Baptism and the Eucharist, and the bond of obedience to the appointed bishops and presbyters empowered by Christ to teach His word with His very own authority.

We truly, therefore, as parts of the whole, belong to each other (Rm 12:4). Each of us members of the Body of Christ has a special role and special gifts or charisms to be used in loving service to each other to build up the Body of Christ (1 Cor 12:12-27). We lovingly belong to each other to the degree that we are consciously and lovingly obedient to Christ the Head. ". . . so all of us, in union with Christ, form one body, and as parts of it we belong to each other" (Rm 12:5). The whole Body is dependent on Christ for His life-giving Spirit of love. Yet each part is dependent upon the other, especially those closest to one another, in order to be nourished and strengthened.

COMMUNION OF SAINTS

Thus, as the doctrine of the Church as the mystical Body of Christ developed in the early Church's teaching, so did the doctrine develop that the purified Saints, who have died filled with the Spirit of the risen Jesus, were able to bring healing to others still on earth or those in need of therapy in Purgatory. Christ's power, especially His healing love, not only comes to persons on earth through the living Saints, filled with deep faith, hope and love, but it continues to come to us and those already in eternal life through the intercession of the great Christians who are now with Christ in glory. Within the first five centuries of Christianity this doctrine of the Communion of Saints evolved. It is based on the solid belief that death does not separate the great saints, the apostles, martyrs, confessors, from those still living on earth or from those still undergoing healing therapy after death. This teaching, so ancient in the Church's teaching and devotional life, assures us that all members who are in the Body of Christ, whether on earth or in the life after death, remain joined, not only to the Head, Jesus Christ, but to each member.

We would like to draw out what this should mean in the lives of each and every one of us, namely, that the great heroes, the Saints and also the angels, continue to share in bringing the healing love of Jesus to all of us who are ever needy or broken. These "athletes of Christ" grow in greater love as they humbly and lovingly seek out those in need whom they may love through service. But this important doctrine of the Communion of Saints has great importance also for us in our relationships with our deceased loved ones. They may not be as "great" as the great Saints and angels venerated in Christian piety through centuries of devotion, but they are "bonded" to us personally with very special human ties of love. They have entered into purification before us. We have seen how we are needed to assure them of our love so that they can break down any unloving habits they may have formed in their earthly lives. But they can also help us in the process. Part of their purification-glorification or entrance into the fullness of "the maturity of Jesus Christ" means that they have need to exercise love and thus become a greater loving member in the Body of Christ.

This means that they need us in order to allow their great love for God to unfold and be actualized in a new, expanded, conscious kind of way. They reach out toward those with whom they have been united in love while they were on earth. Let us first consider the great, glorified Saints and angels and see how we can be in communication and in communion with them as they seek to extend the healing love of Jesus to us through their powerful application of the one High-Priestly intercession of the Church's Head. And then we can draw similar practical conclusions about our oneness with our departed loved ones who can also help us in amazing ways.

GUARDIAN ANGELS

Part of the incarnationalism of Christianity is the constant belief held by the Church that God uses His creatures to manifest His perfections to His created children. Out of this basic truth there evolved the doctrine about angels as the emissaries of God's power and activated love brought into our lives. Rooted in the Old and New Testaments' doctrine about angels, the early Christian writers taught that angels are the channels, not exclusive, through whom God orders the course of this created world. Part of the work of the angels, therefore, is to help and protect God's children in order to lead them into the fullness of redemption and citizenship in the Heavenly Kingdom.

Angels show their love for God through their service of other creatures, just as we are enjoined to show our love for God by serving one another. St. Augustine teaches that angels form the Heavenly City of God and this segment of the holy city comes to the help of the other part that is still pilgrimaging below. Both parts one day will be united and even now are one in the bond of love.[2]

As the angels ministered to Christ, so now they minister to Him in Heaven and in His Body on earth. The angels mount up to the Head and descend to the members.[3] Most of the early

Christian writers of both East and West taught clearly that each baptized person enjoys the protection and guidance of an individual angel. The Cappadocian Fathers, St. Basil and his brother, St. Gregory of Nyssa, and St. John Chrysostom, clearly teach that those who believe in Christ and belong to the Church have their own individual guardian angels to protect them and urge them on to good works.[4]

This is a consistent teaching in the Church that God ministers to us on earth and in the life to come through His angels and Saints. Such "ministering spirits" (Heb 1:14) are found throughout Holy Scripture as the messengers of God or powers stemming from God. What is important, without our trying to dissect their spiritual nature, is that angels make God's goodness concrete, both in this life and in the life to come. From Scripture and the writings of the early Fathers we discover angels as God's protection against the dangers of spiritual evil powers. St. Basil teaches that, as cities are protected by their ramparts against the attacks of enemies, so the Christian is protected by the guardian angel.[5]

It is for those who deny the existence and the power of angels to prove that God cannot come to us through the ministry of angels. The teachings of the great writers of the Church hold out to us the help angels can give us as instructors, who lead us on to perform good works,[6] and who intercede for us who are placed in their charge.[7] It is a gift from the teaching Church for us to believe that at our side is God's infinite power, unfolding through the ministry of a world of angelic spirits. In our present world in which we are faced with so many perplexing forces of evil that seem to our human mind to stem from a world beyond the merely material, observable world, belief in the ministering love of angels should not be a childish "cop-out" into a world of fairy-spirits but it should be a grace from God, through belief in the teaching of the Church, that strengthens us in our struggle against such evil. We can learn to communicate with God's communicating love by walking daily in the presence of our special guardian angel who brings to concrete focus our belief in God's ever abiding and activating presence as love in all details of our lives. "Angel of God, my guardian dear, to whom His love commits me here, ever this day be at my side, to light and guard, to rule and guide. Amen."

SAINTS OF GOD, INTERCEDE FOR US

Who, among all the human followers of Christ, continue to be one with Christ and, urged on by His very Spirit of love, seek to do as much good as His Saints? Not only are they one with the Head in glory, praising and worshiping the Heavenly Father but, in that very oneness with Christ, they now enjoy a special role of intercession with Him before the throne of the Father. Innumerable documents, especially tombstone markings found near the burial sites of the early Apostles and martyrs of the ancient Church, bear witness to the belief of the faithful in the power of the great Christian Saints to intercede for those who are still on earth. Pilgrims, visiting the shrines where the Saints were martyred or their remains were venerated, ask the prayerful intercession of the departed Saints who now live in glory through their imitation of Christ in their lives and deaths.

More than any other early writer, Origen of the 3rd century, in his treatise, *On Prayer*, developed this doctrine of the powerful intercession of the Saints. He shows that, if the virtues are practiced in this life for one's neighbor, they will be most perfectly exercised in Heaven by the Saints for those still on earth and for the departed still in need of prayers. He builds his argument on St. Paul's teaching: ". . . that each part may be equally concerned for all the others. If one part is hurt, all parts are hurt with it. If one part is given special honor, all parts

enjoy it" (1 Cor 12:25-26). He believes that St. Paul's words:
". . . when any man is made to fall, I am tortured" (2 Cor
11:29), can be applied also to the Saints who grieve and wish to
do all they can to help the weak members in the Body of
Christ.[8]

We have all experienced how the love of a dear one fills us
with a burning love that cries out to be shared with others in
loving gift. Love begets love. And love shown cannot be only in
words or fine sentiments but must be manifested by loving
service. Such loving service is no longer considered a chore or
obligation but a privilege. It flows naturally out of the new
creation that love brings about, the new state of being love to
move outward toward anyone in need.

How natural is the belief of Christians down through the
centuries, therefore, that the Saints rival each other in holy
competition to bring more of Christ into being in His Body
among the members of the Church Militant and Suffering? In
a way, Mary, the Apostles, the great martyrs, confessors, vir-
gins, all those who have embraced the cross of denying the
falsity in their lives to surrender to the indwelling Spirit of love,
not only desire to serve us in love to know Christ as they know
Him in glory, but in a way they need us, underdeveloped
brothers and sisters, so they may exercise God's immense love
burning within them by letting it out in loving service to us
needy ones. They need the sinful and ignorant who live in
darkness and absence of their Lord and Savior in order to
measure out as it has been measured out to them (Lk 6:38).

Is it far fetched to believe that the Saints, to the degree
that they have died to themselves and allowed Christ to live in
them, go out to all human beings, but in a special way to the
most forlorn and needy, to suffer with them and to take upon
themselves the burden of the weak? They know the Lord, not
by faith but face to face. Yet they go forth continuously to see
the Lord's face in those who suffer, especially from ignorance

and the pre-conditioning sins imposed upon them by inheritance and society. They are now growing in grace and glory, in oneness with Christ the Head, as they bring healing love to the heavily burdened.

Jesus said: "A man can have no greater love than to lay down his life for his friends" (Jn 15:13). As He died on the cross in imitation of the self-emptying love of His Heavenly Father toward each of His children, so His Holy Spirit inspires His followers to become the only sign whereby people will recognize them as His followers, by the love they have for one another, for all persons. If God brought His love to others during the lifetime of the Saints, would He not in an even greater measure bring His healing love to them through the healthy members of the Body of Christ?

I like to believe that we are surrounded constantly by armies of Saints, who are in touch with our needs and by the power of Christ, working in and through their love for us, who can influence us greatly. How practically aware are we, I wonder, though, of this presence of the world of Saints in our daily life? "I tell you solemnly, insofar as you did this to one of the least of these brothers of mine, you did it to me" (Mt 25:40). The Saints see us as members of the Body of Christ. They see what we could be as they humbly see not only what they were in their human frailty and even sinfulness but what by God's grace they have become: divinized as children of God, one with Christ in glory. Devotion to the Saints is devotion to Christ, the Head, who empowers His followers, especially those who are with Him in glory: "All authority in heaven and on earth has been given to me. Go, therefore, make disciples of all the nations . . . and know that I am with you always; yes, to the end of time" (Mt 28:18-19).

MARY, PRAY FOR US SINNERS

Is it any wonder that from earliest times in the Church,

Mary, the Mother of Jesus, the archetype of the Church and of all fulfilled Christians, enjoyed a special place of veneration but also a special power of intercession on behalf of the faithful pilgrims still on this earth? Such devotion developed strongly among the Christian faithful from the 4th century onward as the Church struggled to understand the mysterious union of two natures in Christ, united to the one Divine Person, the Son of God. Mary the *Theotokos*, the Birth-giver of God, belongs most intimately to Jesus as mother to son, as the living member of His Body closest in relation to Him, the Head.

She intimately shared in the life, suffering and death of her Son. The faithful have always instinctively believed that she is now one with Him in heaven, sharing in the transformation of body, soul and spirit through the Church's belief in Mary's assumption into glory. As Jesus is the "first fruits and then, after the coming of Christ, those who belong to him" (1 Cor 15:23), so the faithful believe that Mary already shares in His glory. Part of that glory is a sharing in Jesus' powerful intercession before the Father. As she surrendered at each moment during her earthly life to live according to God's Word, Jesus Christ, so now Mary, above all the Saints, continues in Heaven to surrender herself to implement God's Word through loving service.

Such Christian belief among the faithful of all ages reassures us that Mary and the other Saints and angels now live with full consciousness and understanding of our needs. The Church encourages us to pray to them, teaching us that they are aware of such communication and can intercede for us through the priesthood of Christ, the only High Priest. If St. Paul burned with zeal to win all to Christ (1 Cor 9:22), can we ever doubt a similar zeal and loving concern toward us in our needs on the part of Mary and the other Saints?

Devotion to Mary through the recitation of the Rosary is a traditional practice of piety long honored by Catholics of the

West. In meditating on the mysteries of Christ and Mary's role in our redemption by Christ, we are able to open ourselves up to her living presence and powerful love for us in her Son. If we as Christians are exhorted by Jesus to go that extra mile for a friend (Mt 5:41), how much more is Mary willing to share our sufferings and do all that is necessary to bring us into a sharing in her motherly happiness?

APPLICATIONS

If we were to take this doctrine of the Communion of Saints seriously, we would find it perfectly natural to walk and talk with these beautiful brothers and sisters of ours who have gone before us and yet are ever present to us in our daily needs. Milton expresses this belief in a world of holy spirits, ever present to us when he writes: "Millions of spiritual creatures walk the earth unseen, both when we wake and when we sleep."[9]

In the workings of God we will find, as we perhaps have already, that we are drawn in fondness and "at homeness" toward certain Saints. These become incarnational points in love of opening ourselves to this invisible world of holy spirits. They also come to know and love us with a certain fondness in Christ. The Cure of Ars, St. Jean Vianney, walked in the presence of St. Philomena. Who are your favorite Saints? Why are you attracted to them? How have you felt their particular presence and help? Does not your devotion to them make the entire Body of the triumphant, glorified Christ most real to you?

DEVOTION TO OUR DEPARTED LOVED ONES

If love is the medium or the environment in which we can communicate with those who have departed, then ought we not be able easily to be in "touch" with our departed loved ones? Though they may not be Saints like those canonized in Christian piety and noted for their heroic virtues and nearness to the Lord, yet there has been a very special loving presence of God in our love relationships with them while they were on earth. Not only do they look to us for help in their purification and the therapy needed to burn out the last traces of self-centeredness, but they also have need to show us love, for to the degree in the new life they enjoy in Christ they have grown to become loving persons, to that degree they stretch out to actuate this love.

The love of God in them still binds them as closely to us as before in the unfolding of our friendship with them on earth. This binding love of Christ's Spirit makes it possible for us to communicate with them and for them to be in communication with us. This has nothing whatever to do with the occult practice of spiritualism in which one seeks to make contact with a dead member of his or her family through a psychic medium. Such practices are to be avoided as bordering on the magical and do not open one up to true love of Christ but to the suggestions of a world of darkness. Our desire is to live in the loving presence of our departed loved ones because our faith assures us that they still consciously love us and wish to help us.

The help they wish to bring in their relationship with us is the help of Christ in answer to our needs in Him unto our happiness. Surely if they honestly wished while they were on earth with us to show their love by sharing their knowledge, wisdom and understanding by offering advice, would it be far fetched to doubt that they can still share with us their enlightened counsel now? Do we really believe they love us and wish to show that love now in a far superior way than they showed it while with us on earth? Then we should not speak of having lost a husband, wife, friend, son or daughter, but rather, we should find ways of communing with such beloved ones often during the day as little reminders of them lead us into their spiritual presence.

I remember a woman describing to me how she had felt the presence and protective, active love of her deceased husband once when she was driving on an icy road in the dark of night. The car careened out of control and was heading toward the median of the road into the glaring lights of on-coming traffic from the opposite direction. She cried out the name of her husband and sensed his hand on her shoulder. Suddenly a force seemed to take over the wheel in a gentle way and she felt the car straighten out and begin to move in the proper direction. You have undoubtedly heard of many similar cases of how the name and presence of a deceased loved one called forth aid in some physical or psychological need.

An elderly nun, Sr. Francoise, used to proofread my manuscripts before she died. To this day I don't hesitate to ask her help in my writing. Thomas Merton also has become a companion as I strive to get through a difficult passage in writing. How much more enjoyment I receive when I listen to Beethoven or Mozart's music in a oneness with their living presence. The whole world around us is permeated with the Saints, angels and all our loved ones. Then there are so many other beautiful persons whom we never had the opportunity to meet personally except perhaps through their writings or accomplishments. Heaven will be that inter-mutuality in loving giving and sharing with those who freely have surrendered to Christ. Heaven should begin now as we live the beautiful teaching of the Church on the Communion of Saints. Then death will never separate us from our beautiful brothers and sisters, our relatives and friends, but it will be the occasion to move into the real world and begin to experience the fulfill-ment of the prayer of Jesus that He is continually offering to His Heavenly Father on behalf of all God's children:

Father, may they be one in us,
As you are in me and I am in you. . . .
With me in them and you in me,
may they be so completely one. . . .
I want those you have given me
to be with me where I am,
so that they may always see the glory
you have given me.   (Jn 17:21-24)

PRAYER TO MARY, MOTHER OF GOD

Mary, my Mother and Mother of Jesus, my Lord and my
God! To you I come in humble thanksgiving for your constant
love and powerful intercession on my behalf. I am beginning
to realize that I experience God's greatest, most loving presence in His gift of loving human beings who show me their love
and privilege me by receiving my love for them. I am beginning to realize that love and, therefore, loving friends, never
cease. Love conquers the seeming finality of death as it brings
forth the possibility of new levels of communion.

What a gift you are to me as I can at every moment open
myself to your loving presence! You have intimately shared in
the life, suffering and death of Jesus, your Son, and now you
share in His glory. You are the first fruit of His new creation
among all who belong to Him. You, above all His followers,
belong most intimately as mother to Son, as the living member
of His Body closest in relation to Him, the Head.

Your glory consists in being ever the Handmaid of your
Lord, present to Him and putting on His mind. You receive
His infinite, perfect gift of Himself, but you also want continually to surrender yourself in loving service toward me and all
my other brothers and sisters in Christ. If you on earth lived to
do perfectly God's will, how much more now, Mary, my

Mother, do you want to come to our assistance?

You know and understand all our needs. You act always out of love and compassion toward us who still pilgrim in this earthly exile. You, who on this earth gave birth to Christ, want continually to form Christ in all the children of God which He has given to you.

Teach me, Heavenly Mother, how I may live in spiritual oneness in your loving presence as well as in the presence of the angels and the other great Saints who with you are one with Christ, their Lord and Master. Show me how I can live in the presence of my deceased loved ones and grow in their love.

You and all others, who share in Christ's glory, see all of us pilgrims on earth in Christ and you love us with the love of Jesus Himself. His understanding and love for us are also yours toward us. You see us already as a part, not only of your continued happiness, but also as a part of yourself as we with you make up Christ's Body. You want only what He wants for us. Your powerful intercession is not separated from that of Christ, the High Priest. It is one with His. Your intercession is not your own. It shares in the omnipotence of Christ's intercession.

How consoling, Beloved Mother, that I can always be present to you and my departed loved ones and that you and they seek ardently only my eternal happiness. You are so eager to do all in order that your Son may be all in all in my life. My life will truly change as I live in this active faith that assures me that you and the Saints and my departed loved ones are in intimate communication at all times with me, if I so believe and act on this belief.

You wish only one thing in my life: to bring Jesus forth within me in every detail of my daily life. As I pray constantly, "Holy Mary, Mother of God, pray for us now and at the hour of our death," may I learn to die in this moment to all selfishness and through your powerful intercession experience more and more my oneness with you, the angels, the Saints, my deceased loved ones and all human beings created by God in a oneness with His Son.

May I walk in your holy and loving presence, confident that you will obtain for me the grace to fulfill your continued command to me: "Do whatever he tells you" (Jn 2:6).

Footnotes

1. Much of this chapter has been printed in the chapter, "Communion of Saints," in my book *The Everlasting Now* (Notre Dame, IN: Ave Maria Press, 1979), pp. 88-104.
2. St. Augustine, *Enchiridion*, 56: *PL* 40; 258 ff.
3. St. Augustine, *Enarr. in Ps. 44*, 20; *PL* 36; 507.
4. St. Basil, *Adversus Eunomiun*, 111, 1; *PG* 39; 658 ff.; *De Spiritu Sancto*, 13; *PG* 33, 120; St. Gregory of Nyssa, *De Vita Moisis*; *PG* 44; 337 ff.; St. John Chrysostom, in Matt. homilia; 59,4; *PG* 58; 579.
5. St. Basil, *Hom. in Ps. 33*, 5; *PG* 39; 364.
6. St. Basil, *De Spiritu Sancto*, 13; *PG* 33; 120; St. John Chrysostom: *In Epistola ad Coloss.* 1; Homilia 3, 4; *PG* 62; 322.
7. St. Hilary, in *Ps. 129*, 7; *PL* 9; 722.
8. Origen, *On Prayer*, XI, 2 and 1; *PG* 11; 448-449.
9. Milton, *Paradise Lost*, IV, 677-678, in *Poetical Works* (Oxford: Clarendon Press, 1952-1955) p. 123.

CHAPTER FIVE

HEALING THROUGH CHRIST OF THE LIVING AND THE DEPARTED

John came to me during a retreat I was preaching in California. He was twenty-eight years old, married five years with two children. He complained of his inability to show affection to his wife and children, even though he deeply loved them. When he was only a few days old, he was left by his unwed mother at the door of a Poor Clares Monastery. The nuns handed him over to a Catholic orphanage and after a few months he was adopted by a husband and wife unable to have children. He was thoroughly accepted and loved by them and seemed to have had a happy childhood.

But married life opened scars of deep hurts at having been rejected and abandoned by his true parents. We talked about them, whether he had any idea of who they were, whether living or dead. I suggested that that day of retreat, before our evening penance and healing service, followed by the Eucharist, he spend in prayer, begging that he be given a forgiving heart toward his parents who disowned him. I encouraged him to bring the compassionate mercy of Jesus to them, whoever they were, wherever they might be at that time, whether deceased or still living. He was to write down any thoughts, words of knowledge given him in prayer or pictures of his parents that would come to him in meditation and during the evening service.

That evening during the penance service conducted around an examination of the eight beatitudes when I encouraged the retreatants, if they so wished, to pray aloud for forgiveness and healing in regard to certain painful relationships, I heard him pray aloud for forgiveness and healing of the anger he had felt for his parents because of their having rejected him. I had a picture of his father, a soldier at the time, who had had a stormy love affair with the mother and left shortly after for Korea. I saw him dead in battle, never having known about the pregnancy. The mother, full of fear and without money, acted in haste to hide her identity and yet to give the child a life she felt she could not have given him.

During the Eucharist he felt an overwhelming peace come over him as he accepted God's infinite love for him through Christ in Holy Communion. Tears poured profusely from him as he accepted Christ's love that enabled him to forgive his rejecting parents and to accept the God-like love of the parents who adopted him.

Six weeks after that retreat he wrote to tell me how freed he had become to love his wife and children in a new peace and joy. He also experienced a new and constant closeness to two persons, his actual parents, to whom he had given concrete names and in whose presence he continued to show his new founded love for them.

WE ARE NOT ISLANDS

We have already dealt with certain love relations as seen from the point of view of the departed in Purgatory who were able to be helped and healed by the love of those still living. Through faith in God's revelation, known through the Church's tradition, we established that there can be contact between the living on earth and the departed. We saw the Church's constant teaching and practice concerning the value of prayers, alms and the offering of the Divine Liturgy. It is both human and divine love that can bring healing to the deceased.

It follows that we can and should pray for the departed. What we would like to stress in this present chapter is that we, the living, can be healed of the hurts received from our own ancestors, from whose blood line we have stemmed, as well as from other deceased persons who in any way have had a negative influence on us. And not only can we be healed, but our healing is quite dependent upon the forgiving love that we extend to those same deceased persons who have set up within us negative forces that have crippled us for many years of our human existence. God calls us to be a healing force in their existence by our acceptance of God's forgiving love in Christ and our application of that love to the brokenness of those departed.

It was the poet, John Donne, who understood so well how intermeshed we are with others, both living and dead, in society. We both grow and are hindered from growing in a society for we cannot exist except in such a gathering of others upon whom we are dependent for our physical, psychic and spiritual development. St. Paul wrote: "The life and death of each of us has its influence on others" (Rm 14:7). With Tennyson's hero, Ulysses, you and I can admit that in all our relations from the first moment of our waking consciousness until this moment and even to the end of our earthly existence and on into the life that awaits us, "I am a part of all that I have met."

Today micro-biology confirms this inter-dependence (both for good and evil, as the Church has always taught) on others in all our relationships. We inherit in birth not only the values of our parents but through them the values of generations and generations that preceded them. Each of the 100 trillion cells in our body contains about 100,000 different genes composed of *DNA* (deoxyribonucleic acid). Each *DNA* molecule stores coded information to be used to sustain and duplicate itself. Such dependency upon our parents who channel into our genetic programming a long, ancestral line links us somehow all the way back to the first human beings. You and I receive not only similar physical traits from our ancestors but we are also the recipients of much of their positive and negative qualities. We do share today in their brokenness even before we have seen the light of day. And we will carry into eternal life much of that brokenness unless while in this life on earth we can bring God's healing power to transform such negativity into new life.

HEALING THE FAMILY TREE

I have often had the joy of bringing persons to the healing power of the Eucharist. In order that the living may be healed of the hurts inflicted by their ancestors and that the deceased might likewise be healed, we offer the Eucharist for and with them and our spiritual bonds with them and God are deepened. The English psychiatrist, Dr. Kenneth McAll, confirms my own experience in this area by his many years of administering healing to such individuals through the Eucharist, offered up for the deceased. He describes his amazing apostolate as a Christian medical doctor and psychiatrist in his book: *Healing the Family Tree.* [1] After serving as a physician in China for several years before World War II, where he dramatically encountered the world of good and evil spirits among the Chinese, he returned to England to study psychiatry in order to see whether he could bring new methods of treating the psychically disturbed and sick.

He found that spirits from the world beyond seemingly exercised an influence upon the living. With careful and often painful analysis of the histories of his patients and with the building up of trust between him and the patients, he was able to lead them into healings that centered on the cutting of any bonds they may have had with a controlling person, alive or dead, through their wholehearted forgiveness and most importantly through the transfer of such control to Jesus Christ. This release of the dominating control of any living or deceased person over another through complete forgiveness and the bringing of the healing love of Jesus Christ to that relationship was brought about through the celebration of a eucharistic service.

Dr. McAll relates in the same place the following extraordinary example of the effectiveness of prayer for one held in mental bondage by some inexplicable evil force. Claudine was fifty years old and had spent twelve years under constant supervision in a mental hospital, suffering from chronic schizophrenia. No treatment or drugs could change her violent temper or alter her delusional state of mind. Doctors operated on her and further deterioration followed. Claudine lost her power of sight and speech and most of her hair. She was allowed to vegetate until one day she was permitted to spend a day and a night with her family. Dr. McAll was asked to see her. Not knowing what to do, he prayed aloud, trying to listen for the Lord's guidance and to seek forgiveness for man's destruction of an innocent human being. All present said the Lord's Prayer together with the final plea, "Deliver us from evil."

The next morning, Dr. McAll states, the family was awakened by her shouting, "Come and look at me!" She who hadn't spoken for years had regained her speech, and her sight along with the growth of a quarter-inch of hair during the night. The secret of this healing may very well be sought in the doctor's Christ-like compassion for her. He identified completely with the feelings which Jesus had when confronted by a leper (Mk 1:41), and he sought only to do Christ's will on behalf of this unfortunate person.[2]

JESUS HEALS

Like Dr. McAll, I have found that persons suffering great physical and psychological brokenness, received from blood-related ancestors or from deceased persons outside of the bloodline, can often be helped when the following steps are used.

1. A prayer at the beginning of the celebration of the Divine Liturgy invoking Christ's power to deliver the patient from the binding evil. This necessitates a firm belief that the risen Lord Jesus has been given by His Father all power over all evil. God wants "all things to be reconciled through him and for him, everything in heaven and everything on earth, when he made peace by his death on the cross" (Col 1:19-20).

2. Through the selection of prayers and readings from Scripture those assisting at such a healing are brought into God's infinite love and forgiveness for the living and deceased who may have been the reason for such pain inflicted upon the party seeking healing. How many have inherited a tendency toward a life of alcoholism from parents who themselves drank excessively? A mother's use of drugs during the pregnancy can also be the cause of a child's being burdened for life and hence in need of prayer in a given healing service. The controlling force of an ancestor who practiced some form of occultism is likewise often evident in the life of some innocent descendant.

This step is very demanding: to be brought into a love that is a sharing of the forgiving love of Jesus on the cross, ready to bear all to gain health and salvation for all mankind. No matter how deep may be the wounds of such hurts and pains, we are to love the sinner, even though we cannot approve of the sin. Jesus tied healing and the granting of all our prayers to our

readiness to forgive others who have injured us: ". . . everything you ask and pray for, believe that you have it already, and
it will be yours. And when you stand in prayer, forgive whatever you have against anybody, so that your Father in heaven
may forgive your failings too" (Mk 11:24-25).

3. At the time of receiving the Lord Jesus in the
Eucharist, let the celebrant and all others present pray
earnestly for the entire family and all who have been hurt by
anyone in touch with any member of that family. I encourage
the persons in attendance to enter into a time of mental prayer
as all present seek to let the love of Jesus flow out from them
into those in need of healing, present or absent, and into those
in this life or the next who in any way were responsible for the
sufferings and pains inflicted upon those seeking in this
service a healing.

Many times someone in the group will be given a word of
knowledge. Another will be granted an intellectual vision of
the cause of the sickness or suffering with the Lord granting a
healing. I usually ask a few with me to lay hands on the
suffering ones and to administer an anointing with blessed oil.
The results have occasionally been very dramatic; at other
times the service merely provided an opening to a continued
and gradual healing that called the ones seeking the breaking
of the control over them to exercise an ongoing faith in the
healing power of Christ in the Eucharist.

NOT SPIRITUALISM

Christians are aware of God's injunctions against invoking
the spirits of the dead. Is this healing of ourselves from effects
caused us by deceased ancestors or others who have exercised a
negative, controlling power in our lives not a bit "spooky"? Are
we not entering here into dangerous and troubled waters? We
are forbidden to open ourselves consciously or unconsciously

and to passively surrender ourselves to the control of spirits.
To surrender out of a desire to obtain favors, power, or success
from such human or demonic spirits is to enter into idolatry by
intimating that some spirits are more powerful than God. To
surrender to them out of fear is also to deny our faith in God's
forgiving love and the power of Christ to deliver us from all
sources of such evil.

But we are clearly enjoined by God in Scripture and
through the Church's practice of praying for the departed to
intercede for the dead and to help bring to others God's
healing power. When we offer forgiveness to those departed
or still living in the name of Jesus Christ, we are acting as His
true disciples. The early Church believed strongly, as we profess in the Apostles' Creed, that Jesus "descended into Hell"
and there in the underworld He brought the good news to
those still in need of salvation: ". . . he went to preach to the
spirits in prison" (1 P 3:19). "And because he is their judge too,
the dead had to be told the Good News as well . . ." (1 P 4:6).

The Church has understood these texts to mean that
those Christians who believe in the risen Lord can by love in
prayer bring salvation and healing to those who have died. If
we can apply the merits of Jesus to the dead and assist to bring
them into greater health, then we can be healed also as they are
healed in their relationships to us.

The power of Christ is infinite and can break the bondage
in which the departed or those still on earth find themselves
through a bloodline relationship or through any other related-
ness that has hindered the fullness of God's power to operate
in those lives. We may not always be aware in a reflective way of
the factors that cause such bondage. But faith in the power of
Christ should fill us with hope that healing is possible if we
come to Him in humility and confidence to put on His heart of
forgiving love toward all who have hurt us in any way.

It is a great mystery demanding deep, child-like faith in

the Lord's power to span the abyss separating the living and the departed, the good and the evil. He can touch us who still suffer from our past relationships with the departed and He can also heal the departed as well. But it is a constant occurrence within the lives of Christians who rely on Christ's healing power to touch the separated, the living and the dead, the pained and broken in both worlds that healings do take place. The secret is believing faith, humility in holding out our forgiving love to those who have scarred us and a view of oneness in that reconciling love of the Spirit of the risen Lord.

PRAYER TO JESUS FOR HEALING
OF THE LIVING AND THE DEAD

Lord, Jesus Christ, we gather in Your precious name and in Your risen presence. You have given Yourself to us as our food and drink in this eucharistic celebration. United in Your Body we come now to beg Your healing power to come upon these gathered to ask for deliverance by Your almighty power from the harassment of evil forces that hold them in bondage. Deliver them, Lord, from all evil from any spirits, angelic or human, that surround them and inflict harm upon them.

For these suffering who are here present You have died. By Your resurrection You have conquered all sin and death. No evil force can withstand Your power or prevail over Your strength to transform all evil into good. We believe You can deliver these who implore You from any force or evil, from any set of past circumstances that hold them from sharing in that abundant life, the life of Your Father, that You came to bring to us all.

We join our hearts to theirs as we beg You to fill us with Your forgiving mercy. We wish to show that complete and pure love which You showed toward the sick and the maimed, the sinners and those who put You to death. May we know only mercy and compassion toward all who have knowingly or unknowingly injured us.

Enter into the depths of those gathered here in humble prayer and drive out all evil forces that hold them in bondage. Free those who labor under the control of powers and circumstances of the past. Bring harmony, peace and joy to their suffering lives. As You give them Your healing love, may You heal those who have hurt them, whether they have departed from this life or still are in pilgrimage to that eternal life. May we all be one in You as You and Your Spirit are one with the Father. Amen.

Footnotes

1. Dr. Kenneth McAll, *Healing the Family Tree* (London: Sheldon Press, 1982).
2. Ibid., pp. 41-43.

CHAPTER SIX

SUFFER THE ABORTED
TO COME UNTO ME

The woman sat nervously telling me during a retreat how she had migrated to California after fleeing from her oppressed homeland. Without family and friends, she had nine consecutive abortions within twelve years. Bearing such guilt within her, she had a complete mental breakdown. Now she is incapable of holding a job and lives on welfare support. Any extra money she has is spent on making retreats in an attempt to get rid of her agonizing sense of guilt.

A priest, like a psychologist and psychiatrist, frequently meets women wracked with guilt over deliberate abortions. Regardless of reasons given that vary from rape, incest, poverty, the mother's physical or mental health, or simply as a contraception bail-out as a matter of personal convenience, the haunting conscience within the woman cries out in moments of inner silence the terrifying word: "Murder!"

Today 4,400 unborn children will be legally put to death through abortion. In the United States 1.55 million babies are deliberately aborted annually. This would mean that in one year the total population of Miami, Kansas City and Minneapolis would be wiped out of existence if each living person in those cities would stand for an aborted fetus. One baby is murdered legally for every three babies that are born alive.

It was reported in the Wall Street Journal recently that Japanese women are frequenting more and more Buddhist temples where they pay $115 for a ritualized service to get rid of guilt for abortion that rises through recurring bad dreams that come thirty or forty years after the abortion. Part of such a prayer service, complete with homily and incense, is the dedication of small statues ("jizos") on temple grounds to aborted fetuses.

A FORGIVING GOD

Christians, through the revealed words of Sacred Scripture and the teachings of the Church from early Christianity, can have absolute certainty that God is a loving God, a Father whose mercy is above all His works. Who of us have not experienced the lifting off of our hearts of heavy burdens of fear and guilt for violations of our conscience as we pondered God's revealed words: "I have loved you with an everlasting love, so I am constant in my affection for you" (Jr 31:3)?

Jesus Christ, the perfect Image of the invisible God (Col 1:15), took upon Himself our humanity and entered into our broken world in order, not merely to tell us of our Father's forgiving love, but to act out this infinite, perfect love by dying on the cross for each of us. As we look up at our crucified God we have the way into the *heart* of the Father's love for us. No greater love does man or God have for us than to lay down his life on our behalf (Jn 15:13).

With St. Paul we can say in the many crises of life: "I live in faith: faith in the Son of God who loved me and sacrificed himself for my sake. I cannot bring myself to give up God's gift" (Gal 2:20-21). We can accept the guilt that comes from having acted outside of God's love and believe that God forgives us and restores us to His eternal love. This is possible because of the blood of Jesus which He freely pours out on the cross in order to conquer all sin and death in us, including the gnawing guilt of our past offenses.

PRO-LIFE FOREVER

But I would like to propose in this chapter a different approach to the problem of guilt that stays with the woman who has freely chosen to have an abortion. I would also like to invite to a view of faith and responsible love the millions of other women who accidentally experienced during pregnancy a miscarriage and those whose children died in birth or early infancy before they had a chance to develop to any great level of human consciousness.

I would like to call members of the Body of Christ to a "pro-life" vision that puts us in touch with the millions and millions of "infant" lives who died before having had a chance to evolve into conscious loving members of the Church of Christ. Our loving prayers and sacrifices for them can be our positive way of applying the intercessory prayer of Christ, our eternal High Priest, to them in their desperate need for love in order to grow into greater life.

In 1975 Jeannette Dreisbach of Palm Springs, Cal., who, with her husband, Dr. Philip Dreisbach, runs the Center for Documentation of the American Holocaust (which has numbered 11.2 million legal abortions in the past ten years), buried two fetuses which she found in a Lakewood, Cal., liquor store trash bin. She embalmed the unclaimed bodies, placed them in a common coffin and buried them. The prayer she composed for the plaque reads: "Pray that a mother's love be strengthened that she does not turn against the child of her womb."

This chapter has one aim—that a mother's love (and respect for all initiated life) be strengthened by our belief that God gives life only to have that life grow and develop. Jesus describes His work on earth: "I have come so that they may have life and have it to the full" (Jn 10:10).

A CHRISTIAN VIEW OF LIFE

From all eternity God sees each life that begins in a given time and space through the cooperation (at least materially) of a man and a woman. He loves that life from all eternity in His Son, Jesus Christ. He sees it as capable, by being made according to His own image and likeness (Gn 1:26), of continued growth in a greater share of God's life. Yet God gives that increase in His life to an individual human being through other loving human beings. God's love is perfected when we human beings love each other: ". . . as long as we love one another God will live in us and his love will be complete in us" (1 Jn 4:12).

Most human beings, including the majority of Christians, erroneously believe that human life and human consciousness develop only as long as a person lives on this earth. After death the growth of human consciousness stops and the human person is fixed forever on that static level of attained consciousness. So goes the thinking of many of us. Such a view predominates among most of us in regard to any loved one who has passed beyond this earthly existence. We believe they have died. We have "lost" them. We don't feel so bad if they had lived a long and good life. But in the case of children, snuffed out of earthly existence at a tender age (and how much more for the millions of aborted fetuses!), there is a sadness but rarely any hope of the possibility of our contact with them, of our love and prayers having a power to lead them to new levels of human development.

How can children, including those who die in the fetal stage, who die before receiving Baptism, have a chance to develop a general desire to love God and thus reach salvation, either by Baptism of water or of desire? Theologians down through the ages have been placed in a quandary due to scriptural revelation and the traditional teachings of the Church. God wishes all human beings to be saved, i.e., to share in His eternal life. "He [God] wants everyone to be saved and reach full knowledge of the truth" (1 Tm 2:4). Jesus Christ died for all human beings, including aborted fetuses, so that they may have eternal life.

And yet, as the Church teaches, Jesus insisted that one had to be reborn by water and the Spirit (Jn 3:5). To be saved one had to profess that Jesus is Lord. "By believing from the heart you are made righteous; by confessing with your lips you are saved" (Rm 10:10).

VARIOUS SOLUTIONS

Over the centuries Christian theologians have grappled with the fate of such children. One early attempt at a solution that occasionally reappears even in modern times is that of *Universalism*. This, basically, is an optimism that places complete faith in God's power and merciful love to carry through with His salvific will and save everyone. Ultimately, it assures us, Hell and any other place or state of confinement will give way and only Heaven will exist for all eternity. In a word, eventually all human beings, including unbaptized babies and aborted fetuses, will be saved. Origen's theory of *Universalism* (*apokatastasis*), with the final dissolution of Hell and Limbo, has been condemned by the Second Ecumenical Council of Constantinople in 553.

St. Augustine agonized over the destiny of such children. On the one hand, he could not reconcile Jesus' ultimate verdict that in the Last Judgment there would be only Heaven or Hell (Mt 25:31-46) with the Pelagian teaching that infants dying without Baptism went to *Limbo*. Limbo (from the late Latin word *limbus*, meaning hem or border) is the theological term applied to the place or state where those who died before Christ's redemption temporarily waited for deliverance. It also referred to the permanent place or state where children who die without Baptism are deprived of the beatific vision.

The majority of theologians before Vatican II followed St. Thomas Aquinas and St. Anselm of Canterbury in viewing *Limbo* as the state in which unbaptized infants will not see God in the beatific vision. However, they will not be in Hell but in a natural state of happiness that would allow them to experience the enjoyment of all the natural goods that they possess.

It must be recognized that the teaching about *Limbo* has never been defined in any Church document. The official teaching of the Church has been one of neither approving nor rejecting the doctrine of Limbo, namely, that infants dying without Baptism would reach a "natural" state of happiness but would not be able to share heavenly joys with their parents and the Saints.

There have been various modern theories to soften the abrasive teaching of the Augustinian view or even the "natural end" view of the traditional teaching of theologians on *Limbo*. All attempts will remain theoretical since we are dealing here with a mystery of God's mercy that has not been clearly revealed to us by God. Yet there are some essential truths of God's revelation that must be kept in mind. The first is that God is love and that He has freely created all human beings, including children (even in the fetal stage) in order that they may all share in His eternal happiness, that they may come to know and love Him.

In this present order of salvation God works through His visible Church and the sacraments to mediate Himself as a gift in love to all human beings, and, therefore, He seems to "need" other human beings on this earth to bring others to Him. Nevertheless, we must believe that His universal, salvific will can work, not only in this earthly existence, but also in the life to come, in a way that befits His infinite mercy and love.

Second, we must hold that Jesus died on the cross to save all human beings, including children (and human fetuses, already existing human beings). He is the eternal High Priest who is always interceding, not only for the entire human race, but for each individual in particular.

Third, we know that, as we are condemned to such punishments in the life to come not so much by God's vindictive decrees but by our own individual, self-centered choices made during our lifetime, so we enter into eternal existence upon death with the type of consciousness that we have formed in our earthly relationships toward God, others and ourselves. Therefore, we can safely conclude that no one will be deprived of God who has not freely turned away from Him through sins personally committed.

St. Augustine and his followers viewed original sin as a static "thing" inherited by being human. It was like a little black spot on the human soul. If a child died without Baptism, it had to suffer the consequences. An obstacle prevented such a person from "seeing" God and enjoying His presence for all eternity.

Today we realize how important is a loving society, our family, parish, city and country, to the re-establishment of individuals who through lack of love have been deprived of full human growth. How can we then doubt that the fate of millions and millions of unbaptized children and aborted fetuses will rest in the infinite love of God the Father? This will always remain a mystery to us, how loving Christians and other non-Christians who live in love toward their loved ones who have departed this earthly existence can meet these underdeveloped human beings after their death and bring the experience of God's infinite love to them. Why should we not learn to trust in God when our intellects have reached a limit in solving possible problems by a black or white, yes or no solution? One thing we can be absolutely certain of: God is love. His loving mercy endures forever. What is impossible to man is possible to God.

LOVING COMMUNION WITH DECEASED CHILDREN

What applications in the concrete does the teaching of the universal Church from earliest times, namely, that the living on this earth can make contact with the deceased and actually help them to be healed through the love shown them, have for us? It should make it easier to realize that our loved ones, parents, husband or wife, sons or daughters, relatives and friends who have passed into eternal life are not far from us.

My earthly father passed away several years ago. But God has gifted me with such a vivid realization of his living presence throughout the entire day, especially when I celebrate the Mass, that I can hardly lament the fact of his death. Rather I praise God that he has died in the Lord and is now becoming the contemplative that God calls all of us to be. I know I can show him great love and he can experience this and it becomes a part of his greater happiness and inner healing. I believe I have often sensed his intercession on my behalf in unique ways. This, I feel, is because I allow him to exercise love toward me through his involving intercession.

How many applications for parents, especially any mother, to make contact with their deceased children, regardless of what level of consciousness they possessed at the moment of death! The main thrust of this chapter is to call mothers of aborted fetuses to a new responsibility with regard to the life or lives they brought into some sharing of God's own life before such lives were deliberately or indeliberately snuffed out. The guilt that accompanies the death of an aborted fetus is tremendous and can haunt that mother for all her lifetime unless she, in her sorrow for her sin, understands how completely God forgives her in His infinite compassion and mercy.

We love others to the degree that we can love ourselves and know ourselves to be beautiful in the love of God. Other human beings help us love ourselves through their expression of the unselfish love they have for us. But unless a mother who is guilt-ridden by the fact of an abortion can accept God's forgiving love, she will never be able to really love herself or the child that she aborted. Such mothers can waste away crying over a past regretted but the guilt must be given over to the mercy of God.

Then she must begin to accept her responsibility toward that life which she launched into an eternal existence. Wallowing in the guilt (instead of accepting the blame and moving on to a new level of faith and love for the life she brought into being with God's help) will not help her and is not pleasing to the Lord. How much more acceptable to God would be her efforts in faith to make contact with the child who lives in the eternal gaze of God's love! Her Christian faith should convince her that her child has died for the reasons she and God both know, but it should also convince her that she can in prayer contact that child and bring it her great love, the very love of God that is being made perfect in that love (1 Jn 4:12).

Such a mother (and father) of an aborted child, in prayer, should often make contact with that child. She could easily enough give that child a name that would help her picture the child and call it by its name in love. The mother has many ties with that child, just as a mother is linked with her living offspring. She must help to develop those ties through loving attention and caring concern. Should such loving concern cease after death? If we Christians fail to show such love to deceased members of our families much suffering results in the hearts of our departed loved ones as they reach out to give

love and to receive it but find none being given in return
through a lack of faith.

A CONCERNED LOVE

May these thoughts be the occasion to encourage not only
parents of aborted children but all human beings who read this
to reach out in love toward the millions and millions of such
lonely children, orphans in the truest sense of the word, save
for God who in Jesus Christ still extends hands of love to drive
away their sadness at having been rejected by their parents.
Jesus, through you and me as healthy members in His Body,
manifested by the love we show toward the most oppressed
and miserable, again stretches out His hands of love upon such
children and blesses them.

> People were bringing little children to him, for him to touch
> them. The disciples turned them away, but when Jesus saw this
> he was indignant and said to them, 'Let the little children come
> to me; do not stop them; for it is to such as these that the
> kingdom of God belongs. I tell you solemnly, anyone who does
> not welcome the kingdom of God like a little child will never
> enter it.' Then he put his arms round them, laid his hands on
> them and gave them his blessing (Mk 10:13-16).

May you who read this realize how much love you can
bring to the unclaimed millions upon millions of children who
cry out for divine love to come to them through human hearts
who are concerned and loving toward them.

You and I are concerned with doing all we can to alert
people the world over as to the dignity of the human person
who begins the long journey toward fulfillment as a loving
child of God at the moment of conception in the womb of the
mother. We agonize at the crimes of so many murders of
innocent children in the wombs of their mothers, especially

those ever increasing crimes in our country which actually legalize such destruction of God-given life.

But we must also as Christians be concerned, by a lively faith in the life to come and the communion of all human beings in Christ Jesus, to come in love to bring Christ's love to the helpless. In our prayers and during the celebration of the Divine Liturgy we can offer our love united with the love of Jesus Christ, our High Priest, to call such children into a new experience of their beauty and goodness in that love. We can offer little signs of love to them throughout the day by way of sacrifices given them as a token of our caring concern for their needs.

SUFFER THE LITTLE ONES TO COME UNTO ME

Jesus is still exhorting us to visit those imprisoned, not only behind bars, but also behind the walls of rejection inflicted upon them in the early weeks and months of their earthly existence. He is asking us to visit the hungry, those physically, but also the little ones who hunger for human love, especially from a father and mother. So many such children thirst for the milk of human kindness and we can give them to drink. The naked babies cry out to us that we cover them with the love of God which burns in our hearts and which alone can drive out their shivering fears. Many are sick and in need of healing. Only you and I can provide it by giving them the love of God that has been poured into our hearts by God's Spirit (Rm 5:5).

> "For I was hungry and you gave me food; I was thirsty and you gave me drink; I was a stranger and you made me welcome; naked and you clothed me, sick and you visited me, in prison and you came to see me." Then the virtuous will say to him in reply, "Lord, when did we see you hungry and feed you; or thirsty and give you drink? When did we see you a stranger and

make you welcome; naked and clothe you; sick or in prison and go to see you?" And the King will answer, "I tell you solemnly, insofar as you did this to one of the least of these brothers of mine, you did it to me" (Mt 25:35-40).

C.S. Lewis in *The Last Battle* in his *Chronicles of Narnia* has all the creatures of Narnia pass through the door of the stable which is death. All of them must face Aslan the Lion, the figure of Christ. As they do, some of them look at him in fear and hatred and they depart to the left into the black shadow of Aslan and are not seen or heard of again. Others, however, "looked in the face of Aslan and loved him, though some of them were very frightened at the same time."

Those frightened ones must surely include the unwanted babies aborted. They will be able to look into the face of Christ and love Him through the love you and I and many others show those little ones.

> In love there can be no fear,
> but fear is driven out by perfect love:
> because to fear is to expect punishment,
> and anyone who is afraid is still imperfect in love.
> We are to love, then,
> because he loved us first.
> Anyone who says, 'I love God', and hates his brother,
> is a liar,
> since a man who does not love the brother that he can see
> cannot love God, whom he has never seen.
> So this is the commandment that he has given us,
> that anyone who loves God must also love his brother.
>   (1 Jn 4:18-21)

PRAYER OVER A MOTHER AFTER AN ABORTION, A MISCARRIAGE OR A STILLBORN BABY

(In any of the three cases centered upon for healing prayer—the deliberate or indeliberate death of a fetus or newly born baby—there are relationships that need healing. The first and most evident healing needed is for the mother (and father, also) on a psychological and spiritual level. In the case of a deliberately sought abortion the mother will have carried, perhaps for years, within herself great guilt. As she grows in deeper intimacy with God through prayer, the guilt may well become greater. Even in the case of a miscarriage or a stillborn baby, the mother will be in need of accepting God's forgiveness if she labors under any guilt that she did anything, even unconsciously, to have prevented a live birth.

Then in the healing prayer there is need to pray for the undeveloped life that began in an embryonic form only to cease living for various causes. Our Christian faith tells us that life is given with consciousness in the earliest stages of conception. Death on the physical level can come about violently through a deliberate attack upon such a fetus by hands wielding lethal instruments or through drugs. It is faith alone that can help us believe that God and our human love can dissolve the horrendous fright experienced in that moment by such an embryonic being.

It can come about naturally in a miscarriage without any deliberateness. Still such fetal life can be helped through the celebration of Liturgies, through a naming and acceptance by the mother and the family of that unknown member and a prayer committal of such gifted life to God.

Thirdly, there can be healing effects during such a prayer service for the living children of such a family, e.g., a twin born alive after the other member died prematurely, a child born after an abortion or miscarriage took place.

Such a prayer can and should be a continued prayer of healing for all concerned as well as a continued love expressed frequently in remembered union with the departed one.)

Dear triune God, Father, Son and Holy Spirit. We gather around Your altar in the celebration of the Passover mysteries of Your Son. Jesus the Lord has come to us as our food and drink. He calls us together in faith, hope and love to pray with confidence that whatever we ask in His name, we will receive.

Triune Community of love, we lift up your servant, the mother who seeks your healing love. She humbly begs your forgiveness and mercy for any consent she may have given to the death of her child. May the sacrifice of Christ on the cross blot out from her heart any sin or guilt that might have an oppressive hold on her. Fill her with great love at this moment, love for You, love for the gift of that baby which You so tenderly placed into her womb and lovingly fashioned on its way to new life, and love for herself so she can accept herself as worthwhile.

We raise up to You her baby through the Guardian Angel to whom You entrusted that new life. In prayer we call that child by the name chosen by the mother and beg Your Spirit of love to pour Your love into its heart. Let that love drive out all shuddering fear and dread, the frustrating sense of wandering, incompleteness and loss of identity. Receive this life which You knew from long ago in the words of Jeremiah, "Before I formed you in the womb I knew you; before you came to birth I consecrated you" (Jr 1:5).

May Your life in that child spring forth into ever greater levels of consciousness as it experiences itself in Your love through us praying with and for its earthly family. May the Angels and Saints join their love with others as they lead it into a new sharing in the Body of Christ.

We lift up those children of that blood-line who may have suffered by being born after an abortion or miscarriage. If there is a twin that experienced the death of his/her brother or sister, may Your healing power deliver that living person from such a deep-rooted trauma. For the children born into a family that experienced such an unfortunate death, may they be healed of any sense of fear, anger, sadness or general frustration and confusion that might be lodged within their hearts.

We thank you, God, Father, Son and Holy Spirit, for Your infinite, merciful love. May we continue to bring Your healing presence to those for whom we have prayed. May we one day meet this life for which we pray now and together we will sing Your praises, Lover of all human beings whom You have made according to Your own image and likeness, Jesus Christ. Amen.

CHAPTER SEVEN

GOING HOME TO HEAVEN

Have you ever looked intently at your favorite cat or dog and wondered what they were thinking? Surely you have shared moments with such an animal that suggested a degree of communication was going on between you and that pet.

I often think that must be somewhat similar to the way God looks upon us, His adopted children. He is the fullness of communication. His Word goes forth and speaks so clearly and powerfully of God's beauty and love for us. We, like a pet animal, strain to break through to a new level of communication with God. Our whole earthly and eternal existence after death is a stretching out in consciousness, not only to tune in to God's self-communication to us through His Son in His Spirit of love, but also to enter into communion with Him. In that oneness we are to share a oneness with all angels and human beings, animals, plants and all things created by God for our happiness.

THOUGHTS OF HEAVEN

And yet, when you and I try to ponder our future home, Heaven, our eternal oneness with God and His creatures, what strange ideas we come up with. St. Augustine gave the analogy of two horses carrying their masters to a banquet at the King's table. These were very intelligent horses who spoke a special language to each other. On the journey they discussed what they thought would be a marvelous menu at the banquet prepared by the King. They finally agreed that the most perfect meal for their masters would be chopped hay and toasted oats! Their horse-appetites could not imagine anything better.

Aren't we a bit like that when we give a thought to our homeland in Heaven? In a recent poll taken among Catholics by a Catholic magazine[1] 97% believed in Heaven and 83% believed they would "go" there. The same 83% believed most people would also make it to Heaven. What I found interesting was that many of the respondents said that, when they arrived in Heaven, they planned on "hugging God," looking up their relatives who preceded them there and on asking God some tough questions.

Like St. Augustine's talking horses, our earthly values, the things we have considered important, find their expression in our ideas of Heaven. For many of us our worldly values, centered upon ourselves and our sense-satisfaction with no suffering or cessation of such pleasures, determine our distorted views of Heaven. We think of what we are going to *do* in Heaven. If we like to golf, then Heaven will mean never waiting to tee off, but unending matches with exciting shots, holes-in-one all over Heaven. If we like music, Beethoven and friends will be there to perform for us. And, of course, there will never be any cost for tickets or waiting in line, things that we so despised on earth!

EYE HAS NOT SEEN

Our sugary, self-centered ideas of Heaven do not match up with God's revealed Word in Scripture. The essence of Heaven is among "the things that no eye has seen and no ear has heard, things beyond the mind of man, all that God has prepared for those who love him" (1 Cor 2:9). "Yes, the heavens are as high above earth as my ways are above your ways, my thoughts above your thoughts" (Is 55:9).

Although we cannot imagine what awaits us, just as a child in the mother's womb cannot imagine what life awaits it outside its confining existence within the womb, yet from Scripture and the sublime moments of joy we have experienced on earth we can gather some ideas of our life with God that we call the Kingdom of Heaven.

It is important that we ponder about Heaven with clear and correct ideas for we will then be guided as to how we can now best live on earth. Heaven is no "place" to which we *go* after we are purified in the place called Purgatory. It is the fruition of who we have become on earth in our forgetting of self and our living in loving union with God, our fellow human beings and all the other creatures of God. It is a question of the real world as God sees it.

C.S. Lewis judges that "it is more important that heaven should exist than that any of us should reach it." [2] It is surely more important that we be in touch with God's view of Heaven since it is an integral part of His reality for us even now in our earthly journey toward our "true homeland" and that we not place all our attention selfishly on whether we will reach the Heaven we often created to satisfy our own selfish needs.

Any intelligent thinking about Heaven should be along the lines of the revealed Word of God and should be congruent with our most transcendent earthly experiences.

GOD IS HEAVEN

When we strip away all our earthly imagination about Heaven as an objective place where we will be eternally happy without anymore suffering, and turn to Scripture, we find

Heaven as relationship. We relate to God in joy, peace and complete fulfillment. We think of Heaven and see God as the goal of all our earthly striving. He is the complete reason for our existence. The idea of Heaven stresses the fullness of our awareness that God is not only the beginning and end of all reality, but that He is *our* God.

We have been driven by an inner force, a burning, passionate desire to know and lovingly serve God in the deepest intimacy. We were created out of God's trinitarian community of Father, Son and Holy Spirit to share intimately in that very life of God. He who is love (1 Jn 4:8) wants us to enter into that ongoing life of love of the Trinity.

WE SHALL BE IN CHRIST

From Scripture, therefore, we see that Heaven will first be the fulfillment of our life in Christ which Baptism brought about as we were incorporated into His Body, the Church. God, as a community or family, extends Himself outward in an eternal, loving movement of self-giving Persons. As revealed by the Incarnate Word of God, Jesus Christ, that community of life is given to us to share and enjoy in and through Christ and His Spirit. Heaven is the Kingdom of God within us whereby, incorporated into Christ, made really one with Him through His Spirit by an inner regeneration (Jn 3:3, 5), we are able to live in the trinitarian community.

The work of the Son is to lead us to the Father. Through the enlightenment of the Spirit poured out into our hearts (Rm 5:5), we are able to experience this life of God as dwelling within us.

> If anyone loves me he will keep my word,
> and my Father will love him,
> and we shall come to him
> and make our home with him (Jn 14:23).

Heaven, therefore, begins already now as we surrender to our oneness in Christ. In Christ we, who have been made according to His image and likeness, will become more like Him, sharing in His resurrectional glory as we share in a oneness with Him. We are not only heirs of God but co-heirs with Christ of Heaven (Rm 8:16). In Heaven we will be like God by being in the likeness of Christ.

> My dear people, we are already the children of God
> but what we are to be in the future has not yet been revealed;
> all we know is, that when it is revealed
> we shall be like him
> because we shall see him as he really is (1 Jn 3:1-2).

Although we now see God, but "darkly as in a mirror" (1 Cor 13:12), in Heaven we will see Him "face to face" (1 Cor 13:12). God's glory will shine from within us. "But when Christ is revealed—and he is your life—you too will be revealed in all your glory with him" (Col 3:4). We will share in the glory of Christ for which He eternally makes intercession with the Father: "Father, I want those you have given me to be with me where I am, so that they may always see the glory you have given me . . ." (Jn 17:24). We received justification through Christ and His Spirit and we will experience that as a sharing in Christ's glory. "He called those he intended for this; those he called he justified, and with those he justified he shared his glory" (Rm 8:30).

In his work, *The Weight of Glory*, C.S. Lewis notes that Scripture presents us with five images of Heaven.

> It is promised, firstly, that we shall be with Christ; secondly, that we shall be like Him; thirdly, with an enormous wealth of imagery, that we will have glory; fourthly, that we shall, in some sense, be fed or feasted or entertained; and finally, that we shall have some sort of official position in the universe—ruling cities, judging angels, being pillars of God's temple.[3]

FED BY GOD

One of the predominant ways of expressing joy and fulfillment in the Old and New Testaments is to describe a feast or
banquet. Jesus describes Heaven in the parable of the man
who prepared a great banquet and invited many persons (Lk
14:15-24). They were all too busy to come. Such were not to
taste of the banquet while the poor, the crippled, the blind and
the lame were invited to sit at the table. "Happy the man will be
at the feast in the kingdom of God!" (Lk 14:15).

Jesus, on this earth, gives us Himself as food and drink in
the banquet of the Eucharist and thus we have eternal life and
will never die forever (Jn 6:48); in Heaven He will give us "the
right to feed on the tree of life" (Rv 22:14). It is the marriage of
the Lamb with His bride, the Church, and all of us are invited
to the wedding feast of the Lamb (Rv 19:7-9).

We will eat the Word of God, immediately and directly,
but also "contuitively" in and through all God's creatures as we
contemplate them in God's Logos, through whom all things
have been made (Jn 1:3).

The joys of Heaven as grounded in God's Word will never
be found in any isolated happiness but will involve a building
of the Mystical Body of Christ as we experience that we are a
part of God's new creation. In Christ we will reach out in loving
service to "reconcile" others to Christ so that "all things [are] . . .
reconciled through him and for him, everything in heaven and
everything on earth" (Col 1:20).

> For anyone who is in Christ, there is a new creation; the old
> creation has gone, and now the new one is here. It is all God's
> work. It was God who reconciled us to himself through Christ
> and gave us the work of handing on this reconciliation. In other
> words, God in Christ was reconciling the world to himself not
> holding men's faults against them, and he has entrusted to us

the news that they are reconciled. So we are ambassadors for Christ; it is as though God were appealing through us, and the appeal that we make in Christ's name is: be reconciled to God (2 Cor 5:17-20).

The central message of the preaching of Christ is about Heaven, finding God's community of the Trinity living within and around us. We become empowered by that Trinity to bring forth other living communities of one and many in the power of God's Spirit of love. This presence of God as community is already infinitely loving each one of us from within. As we open up to His love and care for us in and through Christ and His Spirit, we are commissioned to go forth, both in this life and in our continued life after death, to bring about a social order grounded on justice and love, humility and meekness, respect for the oneness of all creatures in Christ and their uniqueness in His creation. As members of His Body we will seek always to serve each other's uniqueness in love.

CONSTANT GROWTH

If we ask ourselves what our habitual concept of Heaven is we will understand the degree that we are in touch with God's reality. If Heaven for us is the fullness of God's life that we already possess to some degree now, we can see that Heaven is a process of the unfolding of the seeds planted in our being in our initial creation and in our new birth into Christ in Baptism. Have we not all too often read or heard sermons about Heaven that presented it as a static state, a place in which we will be able to gaze upon three immobile Persons, the Trinity, in what is called the beatific vision?

Rather, we ought to realize from our own experiences in life that both our love of God and of our most intimate friends can never admit of a static condition. We are caught up in a

dynamic and exciting process of continued growth in love of
God and of neighbor. To grow in love and to discover
ourselves becoming "birthed" into new levels of our true ego in
Christ through that love which God has for us is to be caught
up within the very dynamic flow of the Trinity eternally moving from silence to speech, from love to action, from perfect
repose and motionlessness to sharing this love outwardly in
movement toward a third. Love is always a blissful tension of
the "already" and the "not yet," possession and searching.

How beautifully St. Gregory of Nyssa of the 4th century
shows us that true perfection is "never to stop growing towards
what is better and never to place any limit on perfection."[4]
Grace or the life of God as uncreated energies of love within us,
both in this life and the life to come, presupposes growth to
accept such a loving relationship with God. It is to accept the
invitation to move constantly toward God into a greater oneness and intimacy. St. Gregory gives us two reasons why our
progress toward God can never come to an end. The first
reason is that Beauty, God Himself, is infinite. How can we
ever grasp God in the vice of our own puniness and believe that
He remains as we have grasped Him?

The second reason is that the Beautiful is of such a nature
that the desire for it can never be really satisfied.[5] As we
contemplate the infinite beauty of God in Himself (which will
be a more direct and intuitive experience in Heaven than
anything experienced on earth) with His beauty shining
"diaphanously" through His creatures and as we see Him
through hearts that are purified of selfishness, we will be
driven on by the Holy Spirit to desire more and more to be one
with that eternal Beauty. There will be an "ever-new yearning
for that which lies ahead," as St. Gregory of Nyssa writes,[6] so
that our desires will never reach full and static satisfaction.

This is why the Dutch theologian, Piet Schoonenberg, and
many other modern theologians insist on growth in Heaven:

A certain growth also remains possible in the final fulfillment. Otherwise we would perhaps cease to be human. Just as life constantly rediscovers itself from the past into the future, so we shall constantly rediscover our past and present in and from God in new and surprising ways.[7]

ETERNAL LIFE NOW

What follows from the knowledge that in Heaven we will always live in a process of continued growth, in a stretching out to live in greater unity with God, neighbor and the entire, created world through greater loving service? The first, most immediate application links Heaven with our resurrection in Christ. But the Good News is that Jesus releases His Spirit within our whole being so, even now in this life, you and I can share in His resurrection.

We recite in the Apostles' Creed: "I believe in the resurrection of the body and life everlasting." St. Paul could not envision immortality separated from the resurrection of the body. His whole preaching was permeated by his strong conviction that, as Jesus has risen from the dead and now lives within the individual Christian and the Church, the Body of Christ, so we Christians even now share in His victory over sin and death.

Death is still a reality for us. It holds a power over us to eat away the eternal life Christ has given us. Yet if today we live "in Christ," not only does death have no victory over us (1 Cor 15:55), but it can become in our conflicts, temptations and struggles an occasion for salvation and a greater oneness with the Lord.

The vision of the resurrection of Jesus as touching His believers which we find in the New Testament writings and the teaching of the early Christian writers means that *today*, in this very moment, you and I are entering into an ever greater sharing in Christ's resurrection. The resurrection of our "body," of the entire earthly person that we are now, is taking place in this moment as we surrender to the lordship of the risen Jesus. In a sense, therefore, Heaven also as a state of sharing in God's everlasting life and seeing God in all things is connected vitally in this moment with our sharing in Christ's resurrection.

Now is the moment of salvation, as St. Paul taught (2 Cor 6:2). It is the only time and place in which you and I are to encounter the "raising" power of the risen Lord. It is the time in which we are to enter into His glory and share in the glory of His angels and Saints who exist already in that state of Heaven. The goal of all our attempts to embrace goodness, to live in love, the end of our pilgrimage and our coming home, is a state already being enjoyed now. Yet the excitement that has us striving so, in the next moment, is the awareness that a greater fullness awaits us still.

Even if you and I do not understand what Heaven will be like and what kind of resurrected bodies we will possess then, we can strongly believe and even now act on that belief just as we may not understand the development of a seed and the fully grown plant or the fruit that comes from the seed. And yet we act on this process of the "already" in the seed and in the young plant and the "not yet" in the fully developed plant or tree and the mature fruit.

HEAVEN NOW

Eternity is not what begins when our historical time ceases. It is the everlasting time and life of God that is already the new time in which we Christians now live in Christ. This "new time" of salvation cuts down vertically through our broken, horizontal time that is riddled by what Scripture calls "sin and death." This does not mean that the old time is destroyed, that Heaven's "time" is the only time we now live in. This old time is being transformed within the context of our daily, human situation. The very broken, fragmented, moment-by-moment suffering in separation and alienation of ourselves from God and from one another is the setting for a "heavenly" encounter with the risen Lord and His Spirit. Jesus Christ in glory enters at every moment into our broken materiality and through His Spirit releases that eternal life, that sharing in Heaven which was given as a seed to us in our Baptism.

Jesus is already risen and we sing that He will come again to this earth in glory. He has gone from this world in the sense that we cannot see or experience Him in His earthly materiality as the Apostles once experienced Him. Yet the Good News we believe in, based on the witness and preaching of the first followers of Christ who encountered Him in His risen body, is that He can now in this present moment be experienced and "seen" by faith in His total personhood, somewhat as the Saints in Heaven experience Him, even though it is for us "darkly as in a mirror" (1 Cor 13:12). The Spirit makes it possible for us to experience the presence and transforming power of the risen Christ in the brokenness and the fleetingness of this present moment.

A NEW CREATION

St. Paul insists that anyone who is in Christ Jesus is already a new creation. The old man has become transformed into new life. "And for anyone who is in Christ, there is a new creation; the old creation has gone, and now the new one is here" (2 Cor 5:17). Our response to the fact that we are already a sharer in the resurrectional, heavenly life of Christ is to enter ever more deeply into the risen life of Jesus in this given moment. Our degree of entering into "Heaven" is being determined now as we cry out in a continued "metanoia" or conversion to leave our brokenness of sin and self-centeredness behind and move into a state of complete submission to Jesus the Lord.

"Lord, Jesus Christ, Son of God, have mercy on me, a sinner!" becomes the continued environment of humility and self-distrust in which we beg God's saving love to come upon us and heal us of our selfishness. During His earthly life Jesus preached the Good News and the sharing in His being, having a part with Him of glory and God's eternal life, as the in-breaking into the Kingdom of God. His preaching, healings of the sick and the maimed, the giving of sight to the blind and the restoring of hearing to the deaf, even the raising of the dead to life, were symbols of what He continues to do to His followers who humbly cry out to Him to bring about the Kingdom of Heaven in their broken lives. In His Church Jesus, through His Word and sacraments by the power of His Holy Spirit, is making available to us now a greater sharing in Heaven.

EMBRACING THE CROSS

Such entrance into the Heavenly Kingdom requires the denial of the false self in you and me. This embraces any of the negative elements in our lives that require a vigilant attentiveness and a courageous uprooting of selfishness and a lack of love toward God and neighbor. It embraces all that is necessary to put on the mind of Christ (Ep 4:24) by an inner revolution by living "virtuously" in truth and in love.

This will be expressed in a faithful response to go forth in loving service toward others to bring forth the fruit of love as we build up the loving community, the Body of Christ, the Church (Jn 15:16). This is what it means to "ground" the grain of wheat in order to bring forth a hundredfold (Jn 12:24).

It is to deny the false in our being to live according to our true nature, made according to the image and likeness of Jesus

Christ. It is to press the grapes in order to provide the wine of consecration unto the blood of Christ who takes away the sins of the world.

As we are "turned" in our consciousness inwardly to the indwelling presence of the risen Lord and as He releases His Spirit of love within our hearts, it is toward the entire cosmos that we turn to be Christ's freeing power of love to conquer the cosmic, demonic powers that have formerly ruled human history. Into our hands is given the power to transform the raw stuff of our daily life in a world that is groaning in travail (Rm 8:22) into a sharing in the glory of Christ.

LIGHT FROM LIGHT

As we are guided by the experience of the resurrection of Jesus Christ in the present *now* moment of our earthly existence, we will more and more become aware that we are already in Heaven, living in a oneness with Christ and serving all God's creatures to bring them also into the same oneness. Christ is becoming the total, glorified Christ as we, both now and in the more complete state we call Heaven, seek creatively in love to build up the one Body of Christ.

This Light of Christ, that has become a guiding light within us, is shining even now upon the world of our daily experiences. In Heaven, it will shine forth to be the source of praise and glory to the Heavenly Father which will never know anything except an everlasting increase from light unto more light, from glory to more glory.

WHAT WILL HEAVEN REALLY BE LIKE?

We have already pointed out the innate urge within all of us to want to know the future and what our home in the future will be like. "What will we be doing in Heaven?" has always been a question asked in all of the religions of mankind. The answers vary, even among Christians who have received God's revelation through His incarnate Word, Jesus Christ. Heaven is a corollary, as C.S. Lewis writes, to the essence of our eternal life: to choose God and live in ecstatic union with Him in His triune life.

There can be no Heaven without God. For there can be no fulfillment of all our yearnings for complete happiness and love without God who is love. We have pointed out how part of that very happiness consists in the possibility of always growing in greater love and hence receiving always more happiness. "More ain't enough" will finally be experienced as a non-possessiveness that paradoxically allows us to possess what we have freely given away. The total person will share in the glory of God and that means on all levels of body, soul and spirit relationships.

Therefore, to ask what kind of a physical body we will have and whether we will be able to eat all the ice cream we wish are, in St. Paul's words, to ask "stupid questions" (1 Cor 15:35). We cannot separate Heaven, which is not an objective place that can exist and be enjoyed as a country club, from our enjoyment of God and God in all His creatures. Heaven will never admit of a *stasis* or a fixity in one state of being or activity. It is a state of continued growth and evolution. We will never have a static, glorified body but, as whole persons, we will always be reflecting more and more from within God's glory in loving service toward others.

Heaven, therefore, is not the end of our existence, our finally coming home to rest eternally. It is the beginning of true life, God's life which, however, already has begun on this earth. It is like an onion made up of layer after layer and consists in nothing but circles of layers. Yet with us human beings, to go deeper and deeper into God's love is to make each circle larger than the last. It is a dance that starts even in this life as we begin to love and dance in joyful harmony with another person in love; as we begin then a widening of the circle of love to embrace other dancers. The dance goes on forever; newer dancers join us as the circle of our love extends itself to embrace the whole world of God's dancing creatures.

WHAT WILL WE DO IN HEAVEN?

This is really the wrong question to ask first. The basic question is: who are we becoming? Who are we in our identity, received in true, godly love? We first acquire knowledge of who we are in Christ and then our actions will follow as good fruit follows from a good tree.

Our primary focus of activity will be to enjoy God. This can have very little appeal to persons who on earth have not thirsted for God and have not drunk from the living waters of God's love. Rooted in God's being as the Source of our identity, we will explore the many ways God concretely loves us. We will discover, as we have also discovered to some limited way in this life, His outpouring love, first, into our own life in so many different ways. We will be amazed as we discover—through the therapy of Purgatory and the inter-action of the angels and Saints and our loved ones still on earth and those others sharing eternal life with us—God's constant and very particularized love in this or that moment of earthly encounter.

We will be amazed as we discover the converging of all those love moments to allow us to enjoy God in this *now* eternal moment of love. As we know and love ourselves in God's tremendous and unique love for us, we will still see our love for ourselves, God and others needing development.

Will we know and want to know facts about others' lives? Yes, but only in the measure that we wish lovingly to serve them through such knowledge. There will be no gossip or idle curiosity stemming from pride and selfishness. There will be no misunderstandings, hatreds, fears, rejections. There will be no need to be on guard, to resort to "white lies" or mental reservations. We will live according to St. Paul's injunction: "If we live by the truth and in love, we shall grow in all ways into Christ. . . . So the body grows until it has built itself up, in love" (Ep 4:15-18).

UNIQUENESS OF PERSONHOOD

We will enjoy a oneness with all whom we meet in love. Yet we will always enjoy a radical difference as we see ourselves and also others in the uniqueness of God's particularized love for us and them. His same perfect love will be seen by us as the same love poured out for us and all others. Yet we will see and experience in every relationship God's love as particular in His unique love for us.

We will have peace and joy as we accept ourselves, seeing ourselves in "our" particular place within the Body of Christ. As we can accept ourselves and strive to become ever more our true self by loving service toward others, we also will have a similar peace and joy as we accept the uniqueness of each person whom we love in Christ and receive his/her love for us in return.

We will constantly be excited by the privilege of meeting new persons, making new friends, discovering them as our brothers and sisters in Christ. We will meet persons whom we have known only in school books. Composers known through their music will rejoice to share their new compositions with us. Artists and poets will continue to create and share as we share with them our inner creativity.

Sharing will be receiving and giving always in joyful love. We will see the secret happiness that we unveiled on earth from time to time and will learn that the more we live to serve another in love, the more we receive of that person and God in that person. We give in service not for any self-centered advantages, but only to draw out happiness in others.

WHAT WILL WE FEEL IN HEAVEN?

Will we know our loved ones who are still on earth? The Epistle to the Hebrews describes the Saints in Heaven as surrounding us on earth: "With so many witnesses in a great cloud on every side of us . . ." (Heb 12:1). The Saints and our loved ones now in Heaven know us and lovingly serve us. In Heaven we will know the needs of our loved ones and others on earth and will live to serve them in love. We will intercede in prayer on their behalf. But we will also want in a loving way to commune with them, sharing with them our love, wisdom, advice and whatever we shared with them on earth.

What kind of feelings will we entertain in Heaven? We spoke already of love and the fruits of the Holy Spirit that follow the greatest of God's gifts, love. "What the Spirit brings is very different: love, joy, peace, patience, kindness, goodness, trustfulness, gentleness and self-control" (Gal 5:22). Such feelings will dominate in our heart and in all our relationships. We will not have any feelings flowing out of *sarx* or sinful nature. Selfish anger, peevish stubbornness, isolated self-righteousness will have all been purified in the therapy of Purgatory.

But can there not be a sorrow in Heaven that results from pain experienced for those who still suffer? Such sorrow will accompany our merciful, compassionate love for the broken ones still on earth or in Purgatory or in Hell. We will understand that at the heart of God's very own love for us is a sorrowing when we do not accept His gifts of love, especially when we refuse to live according to our true selves.

In Heaven we will not be tempted to choose evil because

we are now established in the freedom of Christ's Spirit. He has set us free. We will understand finally that true human freedom is to determine ourselves always according to God's holy will. We will no longer sense an "obligation" or experience a pull to turn away from doing God's commands. There will only be the privilege of acting according to who we truly are in God. We will not only readily embrace God's commands but we will also seek at every moment to do God's every wish for us. Our lives will be totally centered on God as the center of our being, of our every thought, word, deed, wish.

CATS AND DOGS IN HEAVEN?

Is Heaven only for God, angels and human beings or will we meet again our favorite cat or dog or pet turtle? God has created all things to give Him glory. He never creates to destroy but only to become more resplendent in mirroring forth God's participated perfections. "Yahweh, what variety you have created, arranging everything so wisely: Earth is completely full of things you have made" (Ps 104:24). "Yahweh, protector of man and beast, how precious, God, your love!" (Ps 36:6). C.S. Lewis says that animals are saved and enter into the joys of Heaven through their masters.[8]

But why cannot God raise up all the animals, the wild and the domesticated, and make them still present to us in Heaven that we may have stewardship over them and discover more of God's perfections than we discovered through the limited animals we encountered on earth? God surely can do anything. If our favorite cat or dog reflected God's glory and brought us so much joy and a sense of the presence of God's goodness in His gift of that animal, why should not God continue to reveal His beauty in the many other animals and plants and stars and oceans and mountains that we have not yet beheld, bathed in God's beauty and participated goodness?

God gave us charge over all creatures that exist below us. Therefore, we should expect in Heaven, not an old-folks' home of inactive human beings, but a continued creativity between human beings and the world of God's created beauty in all animate creatures, (animals, birds, fish, plants, etc.) and in those we call "inanimate" beings, even though we will then see them as expressions of God's vital energy, always in movement toward greater union, toward more complex consciousness.

Our pet animals will represent the initial sources of heavenly knowledge for us as we find in them something of God in their participated beauty of their Creator. We will extend the appreciation of that beauty as we grow in the discovery of God's beauty in other animals. We will "domesticate" them by Christifying them as we learn to contemplate God's unique beauty in this or that unique creature.

WILL THERE BE SEX IN HEAVEN?

A question that is often asked by earthlings concerning the heavenly life is: will husbands and wives enjoy a participated oneness of body, soul and spirit as they have experienced on earth in marital intercourse? One must distinguish between sex and sexuality. In Heaven we will not have corporeal bodies. We will, however, be totally ourselves, male or female as the case may be, living with glorified body, soul and spirit relationships. We will be united in a special love for our husbands, wives and friends. Indeed, in every look, word (spoken or unspoken), and touch, we will grow toward a more intimate union of love. In this life we, at least intellectually, so easily separate sex from our total sexual being and relegate sex to the merely genital.

In Heaven there will be no separation of spiritualized body, soul and spirit levels as we meet other persons on the deepest levels of love. The intimate joys of oneness that we experience with our beloved, in marital intercourse if we have been married, will not only be recalled but will be enjoyed in a more intense and unifying manner than any ecstatic union attained on earth. Jesus teaches us: "The children of this world take wives and husbands, but those who are judged worthy of a place in the other world and in the resurrection from the dead do not marry because they can no longer die, for they are the same as the angels, and being children of the resurrection they are sons of God" (Lk 20:35-36). The limitations of matter will be transcended and yet we will enjoy a unique loving union with our beloved in Heaven through the total person meeting the other person totally on all levels. How such special, intimate sexual union without "sex" as rooted in the fleshly union of two persons through genital intercourse will take place remains for human beings to experience in Heaven as part of what awaits them of an unimagined experience that must be included in St. Paul's statement: ". . . the things that no eye has seen and no ear has heard, things beyond the mind of man, all that God has prepared for those who love him" (1 Cor 2:9).

Thus we will have special loves and joys and intimacies such as we have experienced on earth. But these will become transformed in a way that will capture all such experiences of godly love on earth heightened to new ecstatic union, never before quite experienced in such fullness on earth but only fleetingly imagined, of what awaits one in Heaven.

HOW WILL WE BE RECOGNIZED?

Each one of us will always be a unique, yet limited, encapsulated being. Our spiritualized body, namely, our whole being in relationship to other created beings, will not be a free-floating glob of consciousness but it will rather have parameters. Such boundaries will not be brought about by quantified matter but by the whole person, expressing himself or herself through a spiritual body which becomes a transparent mirror of the real person within. That glorified body, now a totally spiritualized human being, will continue to express love toward others through its personal presence to them.

We will possess our sexuality and will be recognized as male or female. But no longer will such signs come from any kind of role acting in society as a male or female, assigned certain things to do through the limitations society currently places on the different sexes. Our sexuality will be seen as a unique participation in God's beauty as we are able to love others precisely as *this* woman or *this* man. Sexuality in Heaven will be seen as an asset to glorify God and to express our uniqueness as a gift to others.

HEAVEN IS A COMMUNITY

Whatever we can say about Heaven and how we will live and act in that state will always be only accidental to the reality that Heaven will be our living in Christ. In Him we will find ecstatic happiness through living in God's trinitarian love. In His Spirit we also will be drawn toward others to the degree that we have found our identity and unique ego in Christ.

Heaven has as its essential characteristic *love*. And love requires a dying and a rising, a letting go of our own possessed reality, a reality that we have created out of our inauthentic, false self, to surrender to Christ's Spirit of love by living for others. As we contemplate in Heaven God's passionate love for us in Jesus Christ, His Spirit sends us forth in humble service to all who need God's healing love.

Heaven cannot be exclusively an I-Thou relationship between ourselves and God. God's dynamic, uncreated energies of love within us explode. Heaven is truly a door (Rv 4:1) that opens before us so that we can humbly and joyfully enter into

God's reality. And part of God's real world, as Jesus has revealed to us, is that God has created all things in and through His Son (Jn 1:3).

We will discover the allness of Christ's Heaven, as St. Paul so insightfully wrote, just before he had died: "There is only Christ: he is everything and he is in everything" (Col 3:11). But we will also discover in our creative actions in Heaven that all things become part of the total Christ in perfect praise and glory to the Father as we join with Christ and the other members of His Body, the Church, to "reconcile" all things to the Father (2 Cor 5:19; Col 1:20).

BUILDING THE BODY OF CHRIST

This is the essence of the Christian vocation and the index of our entrance into Heaven and our sharing in the resurrectional life of the risen Lord, as Jesus taught. Heaven is the fulfillment of the Christian life we have begun to live on this earth. But it is always an ongoing process of loving God and loving neighbor in humble and loving service. Heaven, therefore, cannot be an exception to the goal given us by Christ for life on earth, of measuring love for God by the love and service shown to our neighbor. We have absolute proof whether God is in us by the love which we have for one another. "We can be sure that we are in God only when the one who claims to be living in him is living the same kind of life as Christ lived . . . anyone who claims to be in the light but hates his brother is still in the dark" (1 Jn 2:5-6, 9).

The end of all reality is to live in the I-Thou-We trinitarian community of God. In Heaven we will not only experience in an ever-growing process the self-giving of the Trinity within us but we will also discover the same trinitarian presence in other creatures. Our "discovering," however, will come about only through our cooperation with the Trinity and other members inserted into the Body of Christ, all seeking to build that Body into the resplendent glory of God.

We will burn with zeal and love to bring all creatures into a sharing of what we have received from God. We will be called to cooperate in the creative work of transforming the entire universe into Christ. Our yearning for the second coming will indicate our degree of actual engagement in effecting the building up of Christ's Body.

> What we are waiting for is what he promised: the new heavens and new earth, the place where righteousness will be at home (2 P 3:13).

A HEALING LOVE

The Church, as we mentioned when we dealt with the topic of the Communion of Saints in an earlier chapter, teaches that those human beings who are in glory have a share in the power of Jesus Christ, the High Priest, to help others on earth, in Purgatory (and who could even rule out Hell as a place of frustration where the love of Christ could still be an effective presence?). Our zeal to bring Christ's love through our love in Heaven will extend first to the loved ones God has given to us during our earthly pilgrimage. Grounded in God, we yearn to show more love to other circles of friends, of new acquaintances through the infused knowledge given us in Christ of the hurting members of the human race.

Just how you and I will reach out toward others in Heaven and bring Christ's healing love to them escapes our imagination. But we can be certain that God's healing love and mercy extend for all eternity in a pursuit of His children, especially of those who have the greatest need. The more we are centered upon God and have put on the mind of Christ in Heaven, the more we will go out in search of ways to "incarnate" God's love for others in need through our own personalized love shown them. Surely God wants to bring His healing love to the billions and billions of human beings who have never known the tremendous concern of God in Christ Jesus.

And yet God, poor God!, we are all He has to bring that love to others, both on earth and in the life to come! He who is almighty depends on the members in the Body of Christ to be His hands, feet, eyes, ears, mind so that others may hear the Good News and surrender to its healing power. I believe that God's love in Heaven will make it possible for you and me to be present to any and all persons to whom we wish to bring God's love. I like to think that in Heaven we can walk among the broken ones who have passed into eternal life and again incarnate the Divine Physician, Jesus Christ, bending over the maimed and sick, the mentally disturbed, the fearful and the lonely to heal them. I like to imagine that the quivering lips of frightened children will be soothed to a smile, that the hatred of killers and the prejudices of non-Christians toward Christ and His followers will be dissolved by loving persons such as we, ready to do all we can to help others in any way to become fully realized human persons. How we will do this is not important. The certainty that Heaven is a community of loving and healing persons through the power of Christ and His Holy Spirit is what is important.

Heaven will never be a self-contained, objective place for the perfect but will rather be a launching-pad to perfection sending us forth in loving service to all in need. As such it will fill us with wonder and with awe. There we will experience, even as we do now on earth that when we live in Christ's love, the broken ones will be drawn to us and with gratitude they will ask: "But why are you so loving? Who are you? What have I ever done for you that you should be so generous to me?" Then with all the other followers of Christ we will understand progressively more and more Jesus' words: "I tell you solemnly, insofar as you did this to one of the least of these brothers of mine, you did it to me" (Mt 25:40). They will experience Jesus and the love of the Heavenly Father through their Spirit at the same time as they experience our personal love for them. They, with us, will bow in adoration to Christ, the Head of the Body, as we and other members lead them to the Master. And they shall joyfully exclaim: "We never knew such love!"

This is my vision of Heaven. God as love, but experienced as love in our loving one another. And that Heaven is already ours when we love one another, not only as Christ loves us, but in the very love of Christ, His Spirit. No more beautiful vision of Heaven to my mind has been written than that found in the second to the last chapter of the Book of Revelation. It summarizes what my poor words have feebly expressed in this chapter.

> Then I saw a new heaven and a new earth;
> the first heaven and the first earth had disappeared now,
> and there was no longer any sea.
> I saw the holy city, the new Jerusalem,
>   coming down from God out of heaven,
> as beautiful as a bride all dressed for her husband.
> Then I heard a loud voice call from the throne,
> 'You see this city? Here God lives among men.
> He will make his home among them; they shall be his people,
> and he will be their God;
> his name is God-with-them.
> He will wipe away all tears from their eyes;
> there will be no more death,
> and no more mourning or sadness.
> The world of the past has gone.'
> Then the One sitting on the throne spoke:
> 'Now I am making the whole of creation new,' he said.
> 'Write this: that what I am saying

is sure and will come true.'
And then he said, 'It is already done.
I am the Alpha and the Omega,
the beginning and the end.
I will give water from the well of life
free to anybody who is thirsty:
it is the rightful inheritance of the one who proves victorious:
and I will be his God
and he a son to me' (Rv 21:1-7).

PRAYER TO THE MOST HOLY TRINITY

Father, Son and Holy Spirit, I come in humble adoration to praise You and worship You, triune God. You have wanted from all eternity to share with us human beings Your eternal life. You said: "Let us make man in our own image, in the likeness of ourselves" (Gn 1:26). You breathed Your Spirit of love into us and we became human beings, empowered by Your indwelling presence with intellect and will to know You and love You.

You placed us on this earth and gave us charge over all other creatures. Brightly plumaged birds, gazelles that run as swiftly as the wind, raging seas and star-lit heavens were given us as doors leading us into Your presence, now gentle, now awesome in Your power. All of creation is for us to see Your beauty and surrender to Your Majesty.

Let all creatures join me as I praise You for Your desire to share with me Yourself in so many beauties of Your creation. But how humbled am I when I wish to thank You for giving me Your triune community by giving me and all human beings Your only begotten Son. He came that we might have Your life and have it more abundantly (Jn 10:10). He is the *Way*, the *Truth* and the *Life* (Jn 14:6) who leads us to Heaven.

There I am called to live eternally in oneness of love with

You, Father, Son and Holy Spirit. This Kingdom of Heaven already lives within me. For Heaven is where You, Blessed Trinity, are recognized in Your beauty and love and that love is returned by Your children.

O, prodigy of wonders, that God should already dwell within me! When I turn to You in centering prayer, there I discover You, Father, as Light, Son as Light also, and Holy Spirit as radiant Light surrounding and binding Father and Son and my humble self together into an ecstatic oneness that no one can divide or separate.

Heaven, so close, so real already, and yet I see you, God, now so darkly as in a mirror. I stretch out like a blind child to trace Your features in all Your creation. I cock my ear with inner attention, as a robin listening for the stirrings of life in the earth, but how little of Your revelation do I hear and understand?

I am overwhelmed and yet confused that Your infinite love allows You to call me Your child in Jesus, Your only Son. Yes, I am already Your child and, yet, what I will be in the future has not yet been revealed (1 Jn 3:1-2).

I pray for two things in regard to my heavenly destiny. First, triune God, grant me great patience, peace and joy as I make my pilgrimage back home to You. I can so easily become discouraged during the journey. Side attractions can capture my attention and draw me away from You, my center. Above all, I may all too easily forget that I am *now* living in an underdeveloped stage of Heaven, of finding You in all things and all things in You. Help me to see that every moment, with its particular joys and sorrows, pain and happiness, is an opportunity to live in Your reality that I can call Heaven. My sharing in Your heavenly life is being determined in this moment as I surrender to Your perfect love and seek to serve others in love.

And second, I humbly pray for the gift of yearning for

Heaven as for the fullness of life itself, of being in Your loving presence, that still awaits me in its super-abundance.

> God, you are my God,
> I am seeking you,
> my soul is thirsting for you,
> my flesh is longing for you. . . .
> I long to gaze on you in the Sanctuary,
> and to see your power and glory (Ps 63:1-2).

As I yearn for that far distant state of happiness and oneness with You, let me never forget that such oneness should bind me in a oneness also with every man, woman and child for You have made us all to be Your loving children to live forever in Your triune love.

May I never selfishly long for Heaven as a place of escape from building true community in the oneness of Your Spirit of love. May I not see Heaven as a fulfilling of my desires but as a continued process of learning that it is better to give in love than to receive, it is better to bring peace than to want to rest peacefully and undisturbed in a false Heaven. Let me be guided by the reality of the fullness for which You have created me. Let me see that fullness as somehow already present, to be actualized, in these moments given me by You as I journey through sin and death to something always better.

May I measure that *better* life, called Heaven, by the degree of oneness, shared with Your triune family of Father, Son and Holy Spirit, shared also with every human being as I live to bring him or her into greater happiness. May every touch I put to Your material creation make me realize that in loving creativity I am fashioning that New Jerusalem.

May I stand daily before Your Heavenly Throne and with the six-winged Seraphs sing unceasingly:

"Holy, holy, holy is Yahweh Sabaoth.
His glory fills the whole earth"
(Is 6:3).

Footnotes

1. *U.S. Catholic* (May, 1983), "Beyond the Pearly Gates: What U.S. Catholic Readers Believe about the Afterlife," pp. 6-18.
2. C.S. Lewis, *Surprised by Joy* (N.Y.: Harcourt, Brace & World, 1955), p. 211.
3. C.S. Lewis, *The Weight of Glory and Other Addresses*, (Grand Rapids: Eerdmans, 1965), p. 7.
4. St. Gregory of Nyssa, *On Perfection*, tr. by V.W. Callahan, *Ascetical Works; Fathers of the Church*, Vol. 58, (Wash. D.C., 1967), p. 122.
5. St. Gregory of Nyssa, *Life of Moses*, found in *From Glory to Glory*, tr. and ed. by J. Danielou and H. Musurillo (N.Y.: Scribners, 1961), p. 144.
6. St. Gregory of Nyssa, *Canticle of Canticles*, in *From Glory to Glory*, op. cit., p. 270.
7. Piet Schoonenberg, S.J., "I Believe in Eternal Life," in *The Problem of Eschatology*, Vol. 41 of *Concilium*, (Paulist Press, 1969), p. 110.
8. C.S. Lewis, *The Problem of Pain*, (N.Y.: Macmillan, 1962), pp. 138-139.

CHAPTER EIGHT

CHRIST DESCENDED INTO HELL

During a recent retreat to some nuns at their mother-house, I was asked to visit their rather large retirement center to pray over some of the bedridden sisters. It was a most moving experience to enter a ward of four beds with bedridden mental patients, nuns who had lost all contact with reality. They had no perception of why I had come nor did they show any comprehension when I prayed over them.

Their wild faces or silent, blank stares stayed with me for some time as I reflected on the precariousness of our hold on our sanity and our grasp of the real world around us. These patients had lost all touch with the real world through hardening of the arteries or tumors on the brain.

I thought how terrifying such a disease or affliction must be. What a hell of an existence not to be able to communicate with the outside world! To be locked inside the mind with no coherent thoughts, not to understand what others around us want to say. Just a living death without actually dying; no growth, no going forward nor backward. Apparent perpetual meaninglessness!

HELL IS REAL

I received a new insight into what it must mean to be a captive for eternity in Hell. Instead of a mental imprisonment brought about psychologically or chemically, Hell must be a self-created imprisonment in an unreal world that the prisoner himself has created throughout a lifetime. To exist but not to be able to grow into greater being! What a Hell that would be! To realize also that you are not in touch with the real world of God: people, creatures as they have their true being in God's Word. But also that you don't care, for you feel that God and all His creatures who live in His harmonious, congruent will are all marching out of step to your drumroll. You lead the parade; no one follows you, not even the other persons who think somewhat as you do, who have created their own little worlds, each a unique Hell. All claim to be in the real world and yet you and they hate the world you have created. You need a Redeemer; but you are too proud and sure that you are the only redeemer, the creator of the only reality. You hope it will be real; yet you even hate your creation. You follow no one but yourself; yet you hate the world inside your mind.

One of the most difficult doctrines to accept in Christianity is that of Hell. Our preoccupation with the tangible and the objective can lead us to a denial of the world of the invisible, with its emphasis on mystery. The scientific method, when held to be the only approach to the study of reality, makes belief in Hell laughable for most moderns. It isn't so much that they don't believe in a "Hellish" existence as that they are uncomfortable with the idea itself of Hell. The attitude of most moderns in our Western world is: Who could care about Hell?

No doubt Christian preachers have taken the scriptural language about Hell with its emphasis on God's wrathful punishment of those who have mortally sinned and objectivized it into an approach that has all too often become a psychological hammer to terrorize people into a fearful submission to God. With our modern hunger for personalism and intimate relationships in love, God appears in such a presentation as a vindictive, punishing tyrant. Such a doctrine imposed by fear treats us as infants who require the threat of a future life of eternal, physical pain, to manipulate us into avoiding evil and doing good.

Still the doctrine of Hell is extremely meaningful today; more than ever before. It will always be important for those Christians who believe in Christ who, through Scripture and the teachings of the Church founded by Him, has strongly and clearly taught this doctrine, even though He used the oriental imagery common to Jewish teaching on Hell of His day. The teaching of Christ on Hell must be purified from the accidental details of the imagery and symbolism used, in order to enable us to reach the kernel of truth that is ever so real and important for us in these modern times.

I AM FREE

Today as we strive to become more individuated by exercising our free will to choose to become who we wish to be, Hell is the necessary corollary to the fact that we are free persons. We see so much loneliness, physical and psychological, and so many suicides stemming from a lack of love. God is love. He calls us to return His love freely. We see in our actions, more today than ever, how the choices we make determine the type of persons we become.

Through reason, assisted by faith in Christ's teaching on Hell as handed down to us through the Church's guidance, we can get at the most essential elements of the doctrine of Hell. We can discover for ourselves its great importance for us and the many applications such a belief has in our daily life, made up as it is of so many free choices that determine the person we freely opt to be.

HELL NOT A PLACE

God did not create Hell as a physical place, with walls and burning fires that inflict upon the inmates terrible physical, eternal sufferings. Hell is the state of not being one's true self, the person God has gifted with such unique potential. The free will of angels and human beings, of whoever may be in Hell, accounts solely for the existence of Hell. This important teaching about the existence of Hell is a dramatic either/or statement about God's gift to us of free will so that we can *either* freely love Him in return for His infinite love for us *or* freely turn away and live solely for ourselves in isolated selfishness.

We may ask: Would it not be insane to choose to create such a Hell, to serve self rather than God? The essence of this teaching on Hell, as revealed by Jesus Christ, is not to convince us that certain fallen angels and human persons are *now* in Hell. Christ and the Church have never made a definitive statement about the inhabitants of Hell, not even a statement to the effect that there is even one human being in Hell. It is an important teaching to show us how much God apprises our freedom by which we can return His everlasting love.

FREE TO DESTROY OURSELF

We can look all over our life and see many occasions when we were faced with decisions: to live in this concrete situation selfishly for ourself or to forget the pull toward self-indulgence in order to live lovingly to help someone else. If we chose the path of selfishness, we know how easy it became to do it again and again in other situations. We remember our justification that acting in such a way (that really was selfish) was a good, the correct way to act in the circumstances. To have acted lovingly (as others would have expected) was to be soft and cowardly.

Our common human experience should convince us of the truth of the prophet Jeremiah's statement: "The heart of man is deceitful" (Jr 17:9). The doctrine of Hell is very practical. It reminds us that if we act again and again out of selfishness, without prayer and self-examination to call us back to

God's reality, we will be caught in the state of Hell, even now on earth. As we live now, so will we die, unless there be a return to God's love and a sharing of that love with our neighbor.

But more, this doctrine of Hell is a statement that upon death, we become spiritualized persons whose selfish values condemn us forever in an evil kingdom of darkness. In Hell we join other persons who relate toward God, themselves individually, toward other rational beings and toward the entire cosmos in an aggressive, attacking way. All such persons living out of self-centeredness are joined together in disharmony and hatred for the values of God's reality and those who have opted to live by love for others.

THE MYSTERY OF HELL

What, we may ask, will Hell be like? It cannot be a physical location, an objective place such as we would go to in visiting a certain city or country that has parameters, frontiers and citizens living within and taking orders from the ruler of that kingdom. Such an objectivization places the burden upon God to create it out of His purpose to requite His anger by punishing fallen angels and sinful human beings who have disobeyed His holy will. And such a doctrine truly denies the essential revelation of God's Word to us that God really wants and effectively wills that all angels and human beings be saved (1 Tm 2:5; Jn 3:16-17). For God to will the salvation of all men and women is for Him continuously to love each person in a unique, personal, self-involving encounter.

From God's viewpoint we can be absolutely assured that His love endures forever. His mercy is above all His works. If God so loved this world and wished each individual to share His life when He gave us His Son to die that we might have eternal life, then how could God have initiated Hell as a place to punish millions for all eternity and rejoice that His justice would finally be accomplished?

Hell is brought about as a freely-willed state by a created, free, individual, an angelic or human nature who has chosen freely and habitually to act in a selfish way as though he/she were God, the central pivot point of all reality. Hell is not forced upon us from outside. It is like a consuming cancer that starts slowly from within with its lethal growth unto the death of the true life within us. This true life is God's life which grows and ushers us into a greater share of eternal life, God's life, whenever we choose to live lovingly toward God and neighbor.

SIN IS ITS OWN PUNISHMENT

The powerful doctrine of Hell loses its true impact and Christ's purpose is lost when we consider Hell solely as a punishment that follows a lifetime of sin. Seen in the light of the urgency with which Christ preached the imminence of Hell as a reality for every human being, sin and a life of living selfishly become their own punishment. Jesus wishes us to realize that it is we ourselves who replace God's divine life as realized love for us by setting up our own self-love and thus creating our own unreal world. The punishment comes from our unreal world pitted in hatred and obstinacy against God and His loving children.

In Hell one is not only alone in non-reality, but such a person clings in a threatened, hateful, sink-together attitude with others of a similar mind-set. What can be said about the descriptions of burning fires as a part of Hell's punishment? The raging fires come from within ourselves as we in the life-to-come experience our utter frustrations at having failed to live up to our tremendous potentiality. We will realize that we were created by God for love and happiness and we will know that we alone are responsible for our own unhappiness because of our rejection of the love of God and neighbor. In that future life of Hell we would know more clearly the truth and see that our having freely consented to sin is our own punishment and not anything God does to us. Part of that punishment would come from the realization that God still loves us and yet we are locked into obstinacy following our own conditioned rejection of such offered love.

That sin is its own punishment would be seen in the inner violence we would continue to do to ourselves by continuing to attack all other positions but our own and yet to know the hopelessness of our own position. We would find ourselves running from God and true reality and would have the feeling of going farther into darkness but not being able to stop running headlong into continued chaos and more frustration. If Heaven is a continued growth in self-giving love toward God and others, then Hell would be a continued growth of experiencing more and more the mounting frustrations that an individual alone freely has set into operation by his turning from love for God and neighbor.

WHY CANNOT GOD FORGIVE THOSE IN HELL?

If God is all-loving, why can He not give those in Hell another chance? In the history of Christianity down through the ages this stress on God's goodness over man's sinfulness in willing to create a hellish existence of selfishness has brought forth a faulty teaching known as *Universalism*. Such a teaching, following that of the 3rd century teacher of Alexandria, Origen, emphasizes the overwhelming love and mercy of God as capable eventually of "converting" even the heart of Satan himself. In such a doctrine God will always continuously extend an opportunity for those in Hell eventually to win Heaven, and Hell would freeze over and dissolve out of existence.

There are many conciliar documents that deny universalism and insist on the impossibility of a fallen angel or human being of ever leaving such a state as Hell. The Councils of Florence, Lateran IV, Trent and the Athanasian Creed all speak of everlasting fire in Hell and perpetual punishment for the wicked in Hell.[1] This was the manner in which the Church Fathers interpreted Christ's teaching as an insistence upon man's inability by his/her own power to change a lifetime of choices to live selfishly. Jesus was a preacher insisting that His hearers come to decisions in the *now* moment to live lovingly and be converted *now*, not after an "eternity" of self-inflicted punishments, called Hell.

Jesus' constant preaching in parable form about the Heavenly Father's infinite mercy and all of Scripture's insistence on God's mercy as everlasting and above all His works should convince us that God will never cease to love us. In this life He never gives up on us. But in this life and in the life to come, if we insist upon using our free will selfishly to fashion a state of being that freely excludes God's love from being experienced by us, then God will respect our choices. He stands at the door and seeks entrance by knocking. But it is we who hold the key to open the door from within (Rv 3:20).

WILL HELL EXIST FOREVER?

The symbols and images used in Scripture and in the sermons of Christ in describing the punishments of Hell imply that this state of existence will last forever. Scholars today point out the need to see the images and symbols as just that, namely as images used to express an awesome mystery: God's everlasting love for each human being vs. man's use of his own free will to subvert God's desire that all men be saved. Eternity cannot be adequately measured merely in terms of our earthly time being extended to infinity.

Can we really objectivize the mystery of such an interaction between God and us human beings? Can we ask whether there will be persons who will suffer eternally in Hell? In his fantasy, *The Great Divorce*, C.S. Lewis asks the Scotch spiritual writer George Macdonald this question. We should heed his reply:

> . . . all answers deceive. If ye put the question from within Time and are asking about possibilities, the answer is certain. The choice of ways is before you. Neither is closed. Any man may choose eternal death. Those who choose it will have it. But if ye are trying to leap on into eternity, if ye are trying to see the final state of all things as it *will* be (for so ye must speak) when there are no more possibilities left but only the Real, then ye ask what cannot be answered to mortal ears. Time is the very lens through which ye see—small and clear, as men see through the wrong end of a telescope—something that would otherwise be too big for ye to see at all.[2]

Thus the mystery of God's everlasting love and universal salvific will must be seen together in such a way as not to take away the power of man's individual free will to receive or to refuse this gift of God's invading love. From God's viewpoint His love is always there, as the sun is always shining, giving light and warmth. Man, so long as he is on earth, always retains the awesome power to choose either to remain in darkness, absent from God's loving light or to accept the light and live forever in His love.

From the viewpoint of angels and human beings who freely choose the hellish condition, there is no salvation, no chance of changing. We must resist, however, with Christ and the teaching of the Church, to declare in any objectivized way that specific persons are in Hell forever or that their sufferings will be eternal. When Jesus was asked whether only a few would be saved (Lk 13:23), He simply replied: "Try your best to enter by the narrow door."

For us making the great decision, and for Christ and for

every teacher concerned with exhorting human beings in this life to choose rightly, Hell is possible, even now. From one point of view, that of our human free choices, it is eternal. There is something as real in the terrifying self-inflicted punishments as everlasting fire. It is irreversible. It defies the law of contradiction. We cannot freely choose and at the same time not freely choose. If we choose to live by selfishness, then we at the same time cannot live out of loving self-sacrifice.

A SPIRITUAL PSYCHOTIC

Did you ever meet a person who, for whatever reason, was trapped inside his or her own mind, a psychotic person unable to escape this mentally disturbed state to make contact with the outside world through ordinary human communication? Such persons often remain helpless for years in our mental hospitals, not free to choose anymore either to remain in their unreal world or to opt to "come back" into the real world. Pitifully they are trapped in this state of existence, unable to break out of it, yet not living in any real sense as a human being.

So Jesus is right. If we choose to live selfishly, the more we enter into the twisted pattern of living only for ourselves, the more we will find ourselves eternally unable to help or heal ourselves. For how can we even remember what love is if we build around ourselves a world in which the only pattern of value is centered upon ourselves? How can we ever have the power to move out to someone other than ourselves in love if all we have known by choice has been selfishness?

THE MYSTERY OF GOD'S LOVE

But when we ask about the everlasting existence of Hell,

we must also see it from God's viewpoint. Dante in his classic, *Inferno*, has emblazoned on the gates of Hell the words: "Let all who enter here abandon all hope." There is no hope that anyone caught in the hellish slavery of selfishness can heal him/herself. In the past preachers and theologians have often accented the hopelessness and eternity of Hell as seen from man's viewpoint. Thus they have stressed that it is God who punishes those in Hell out of His despotic sense of vengeance. In doing so they truly substituted a pagan god for the Father of Jesus!

We must ever remain in the mystery of God's love and mercy, never losing our hope in what His love can accomplish. His love can do more than we could ever hope for. Yet we cannot conclude that therefore God's love definitely will conquer the obstinacy of all resisting persons and Hell will one day cease: "So, sinners, don't worry! You may continue to live as you wish. God's love will eventually conquer your sins and save you!"

Wrapt in awe that in His humility God loves us forever, regardless of our response to Him, as shown especially in His greatest manifestation of emptying love for us in His Son, Jesus Christ, poured out on the cross for us, we can say no more. We can only thank God for having revealed to us this doctrine concerning the power He has given to us in giving us free will. Hell is no place created by God. It can only be seen as the state of being of those angelic or human persons who have freely chosen to reject God who in His "weakness" constantly pursues us with His self-sacrificing love in order that He might share with us His own divine life. This life is a life of community in which the law of existence is posited on the principle of love or self-emptying.

That principle Jesus preached along with His teaching on Hell:

I tell you, most solemnly,
unless a wheat grain falls on the ground and dies,
it remains only a single grain;
but if it dies,
it yields a rich harvest.
Anyone who loves his life loses it;
anyone who hates his life in this world
will keep it for the eternal life (Jn 12:24-25).

Love of God and neighbor necessitates a shedding of our false ego that has been built up through sin and leads to death, the seeds of Hell and selfishness. To hold on to that false self is to embark on a life of choices that we can call Hell on earth. It is to frustrate and go against the powerful attraction for Paradise which God implanted in our human nature when He created us according to His own image and likeness (Gn 1:26). To frustrate such a calling is for us to deny our dignity and create our own inner punishments and an eternal Hell. To hate and put to death the unreal, false self is to begin the long journey home to our Father's house. There all of us prodigal children can be assured that our Heavenly Father, the Father of Jesus, has always been waiting for our return. God's almighty power resides in our graced free will. He will do nothing to change that. With confidence in us He waits for our return to His arms. The doctrine of Hell is very important. Its teaching tells us much about ourselves and our own ability to lose eternal happiness. It tells us much more about God's everlasting love and His humility to wait forever for us to come home.

PRAYER OF THE PRODIGAL SON

Father, I have sinned against Heaven and against You! I truly do not deserve to be Your child. I know that in the story Jesus told in the Gospel about the prodigal son, the returning son never had a chance to give his speech. The father cut him off. He smothered him with tears of joy, kissed him tenderly and started to treat him as if he were even more loved by the father than if he had not turned away and left him.

Let me finish the prodigal son's speech. "I want to tell You, Heavenly Father, of the Hell of living selfishly for myself and forgetting Your love. How could I have ever done those selfish acts of using Your money, Your talents given to me, my health, my intelligence, my body, my mind, all for my own purposes?

"But infinitely more, how could I have ever used other persons like playthings. I broke them and then threw them on heaps of junk to let them know I thought they were only things, existing for my use. I judged their worth and they better damned accept my verdict! I was judge, and my judgments made reality!

"But what misery filled my heart as I daily built my own created world. Darker became my eyes until I saw persons as shadows. I kept following that thin grey line like a thread that took me into a hideous world of monstrous figures and grotesque shapes. Deeper I reeled from nightmare to nightmare. I paused, frightened. A voice ever so faint told me to break the thread and go back. But I plunged on, excited, afraid, cold and hot, running and falling, but ever deeper.

"My world was narrowing into an imprisoning, darkened chamber. I felt a presence come over me, a voice ever so faint. It told me to follow the light. What light? I searched and found a faint ray of light, ever so faint. I remembered in the warmth of that ray of light what it was like in Your love when I was once Your child. I could not make out the way. There was only the ray that showed me one step in my darkness. I could not run. I crawled frantically on my knees. Forces of darkness kept blocking out that faint ray.

"There it was! No, now it was lost! What agony to feel so

lost in that confining darkness and to wonder if it would be forever! I cried out Your name and the faint ray reappeared. Stronger it became as I cried out all the more! I was rising and going home!

"Forgive me, Your unworthy child. Do with me whatever You wish. But whatever happens, I wish only to love You. Any other choice is unhappiness and Hell itself. Living in Your love is Heaven!"

Footnotes

1. Cf. DS 858; DS 1306; DS 801; DS 76; DS 1539; 1543; 1575; DS 1705.
2. C.S. Lewis, *The Great Divorce* (N.Y.: Macmillan, 1946), pp. 128-129.

CHAPTER NINE

I WILL RISE FROM THE DEAD

What we have been doing in this book is to de-objectivize the great truths revealed to us about what happens to us after we die. To break through a rather static view of life after death as time spent in places called Heaven, Hell and Purgatory, we sought to return to a more biblical concept of the human person.

In such a vision of ourselves from Scripture we discover that God has made the whole human person according to the image and likeness of Himself, who is Jesus Christ, the Word Incarnate. We cannot be divided into separable compartments called a body, a soul and a spirit. The whole person lives and influences in his/her choices the life entered upon after death. The potential to be made participants of God's very own nature (2 P 1:4) extends into the life to come, making life in God an infinite growth possibility that begins with the quality of life we live here on earth and extends into eternal life hereafter. We are whole persons, meant by God's indwelling presence within us to become integrated in all our divinely given powers and to become ever more consciously one with the indwelling Trinity and one in love with all of God's creatures.

We are called by God's love into a greater increasing consciousness of harmony and unity through love, not only with God, within ourselves, but with all angels and human beings and the entire animal, plant and inanimate kingdom.

Life now and hereafter is a process of continued growth dependent on our free choices. The concepts of life and death are complementary and cannot be separated. Heaven and Hell and Purgatory are all quite dependent on our awesome power, given to us by God, to make our own free choices and enter into such loving or hateful relationships with God and neighbor and the created world as imaged by the concepts of Heaven and Hell.

DYNAMIC VISION OF RESURRECTION

All the points that we have considered in the earlier chapters can be summarized and highlighted in this last chapter concerning our belief in Christ's resurrection from the dead and our own personal resurrection. We can approach this important truth (to which we give assent in the Creed, that Christ arose from the dead and that we will also be raised from the dead at the end of the world) from a static view or from that of a process of continued growth, dependent on our free choices both now and in the life to come.

In the static view Jesus died on the cross, that is, His body died, while His soul separated from His dead body and went off to Limbo or some ethereal "place" to preach to those of the Old Testament. After three days His soul returned to the sepulcher to re-enter His dead body and to restore life to it, so that He now had a "risen" body with the amazing power to pass through doors and walls, etc. Such a static view pictures our own individual resurrection as taking place at some objectivized point at the end of the world. Our body will be in some grave. At a given signal from God, all the souls of human beings, including our own, will travel back to earth to enter into those dead bodies and we all will be risen at the same time to enter into the final judgment. Then we will receive our eternal just reward, either eternity in Heaven or Hell.

In a way, as St. Paul realized, our faith in the resurrection of Christ and our own personal resurrection is the pivotal point or cornerstone of Christianity. As we not only believe in Christ's resurrection and our own from the dead but also conceive it, so we will live. If we continue to entertain a static view of resurrection, we will tend to set aside such an important truth, one that should affect our everyday decisions until the end of the world. According to such a view, the doctrine of our own resurrection is not very important and has few applications for our daily living.

But a truer vision of the resurrection of Christ and our own sharing in His glory sees physical death as part of a dynamic growth process that continuously involves our free choices to live what was so beautifully symbolized in our first Baptism: namely, to die daily to selfishness and rise by the power of the Spirit of the risen Lord to live in loving service toward others.

Jesus died as a whole person; not merely did His body die. He *passed over* into His new, resurrectional existence immediately, not after three days—an image St. Luke uses from the book of the prophet Hosea (Ho 6:2). Nor does the resurrection take place merely inside the tomb. It is a process. The total Christ dies. And the total Christ is raised into glory by His Heavenly Father. Love, when it reached its peak in the heart of Christ during that momentless moment on the cross, moved immediately from death in aloneness to enter into a new union with the One He loved always, His Heavenly Father. As a result He can pour out His Spirit upon us and we can even now share with Him His divine life.

We, too, will die. But before we have physically "left" this earthly existence we will be faced with many situations in which we are called to choose freely to undergo a series of psychological and spiritual deaths to our false, unspiritual self and enter into a deeper sharing in the risen life of Christ who leads us into the unity of the Trinity and into a greater unity of love with other human beings. As we live our Baptism, we already share, not only in the sufferings, but also in the glory of Christ, our Head.

Our resurrection is now seen as the peak of our human development. It admits of a fuller manifestation of our sharing in the glory of the risen Lord at the end of the world. But that will only be the result of our present choices based on love that necessitates taking up our cross by going against our selfishness in order to live in Christ and as He lived.

ENTERING INTO THE KINGDOM

Jesus called our sharing in His resurrection, even now, according to the Jewish messianic expectations, our entrance into the Kingdom of Heaven. Jesus preached this as the Good News. But He also knew what was in the heart of man and woman. He preached that both He and His followers were to suffer by living a life based on the principles of the Beatitudes which are summaries of His two great commandments of love: to love God with one's whole heart and one's neighbor as oneself. To such as live this life, the resurrection or entrance into the Kingdom of God would be given.

This Kingdom of union in intimate love with the Trinity would reach its actualization only through the Holy Spirit, given after Jesus died, for only then would we realize the infinite love of God made manifest for us individually in the sufferings of Christ who died for us (Gal 2:20). Sharing in the Kingdom of Heaven is to share already in the resurrection of Christ. Both admit of a slow process of steady growth, dependent upon our moment-by-moment decisions to choose to live in love rather than in selfishness.

The fullness of glory in God's life is already contained in

our original creation according to God's image (Gn 1:26). Just as a seed already contains all in itself yet needs nourishment from outside and conflicts to create tensions if its hidden potential for greater life is to be released, so we need the nourishment of outside love and trials and tribulations to create the set-up for us to choose to accept our selfless God or to serve Mammon, the image of selfishness.

The ultimate power of growth and of producing fruit is summarized by the love of God that is poured into our hearts through the Spirit that is given us (Rm 5:5). You and I are always in need of a continuous conversion. We need an inner attentiveness to the *now* moment, to God's inbreaking with His Kingdom, His trinitarian indwelling experienced in a conscious manner on our part as we choose to accept to live in loving obedience to His will. We need to put on the mind of Christ by an "inner revolution" (Ep 4:23). This means a continued rebirthing of ourselves through the Spirit from above (Jn 3:3, 5).

This is the paradox of genuine growth into our true selves: we must lose our lives in order to find them in God (Jn 12:24-25). It is a source of constant suffering to go against our false ego and make God the axis of our life. Yet He must truly be made Lord over our every thought, word and action. Such a constant conversion to enter into the Kingdom of Heaven or to share in the glory of Christ's resurrection is posited on the threefold movement of all prayer. We are to be rooted in the awesome "allness" of God, in His transcendence. He alone is God! We are His gifts, empty receptacles to be filled by God's goodness. We are to confess with humility and distrust in our own ability to live in God's truth that there is brokenness within us, in a false ego that can at any time assert itself. And there is sin and death all around us. There is sin in our members, as St. Paul experienced and continually confessed before Christ (Rm 7:23). And, lastly, we will experience continually the awesome otherness of God descending into our emptiness to fill us with His immanently indwelling trinitarian life.

WHAT DOES RESURRECTION MEAN TO US?

We can easily handle our personal resurrection if we objectivize it and place it far from this present moment in our actual human situation of *now* right up to the end of the world. Such a truth has no urgency to be acted upon by us. No great choice has to be made in the *now* moment according to its truth. But the reality of Christ's resurrection and our experience of it are inbreaking our present choices to draw us to a decision *now*. God the Trinity in the context of our human situation is now inviting us to choose to be our true self. God always has known and loved us in Jesus, His Word, according to whose image and likeness we have been created.

The reality of Jesus' resurrection ushers us in this moment into a new time, the *kairos* time of encountering God's eternal love as life. It is the "acceptable time of salvation" in which we are to surrender the brokenness of the sin and death in our life through our self-absorption in order to put on the new life of the risen Jesus. This experience of the risen Lord takes place in what Scripture calls our *heart*. This is not our physical heart but our deepest consciousness informed by the grace of the Spirit infusing into our awareness deeper faith, hope and love to "experience the resurrection of Christ," as St. Paul prayed in Ph 3:10. We come to know by God's knowledge that God is our source and final goal. We yearn to live in that reality which is constantly unfolding within the core of our being and we seek ever to return God's love by wishing to live in His holy will.

This is how Jesus preached about the necessity of Himself suffering daily to do the will of the Heavenly Father so as to enter into glory through the resurrection (Lk 24:25-27; Ph

2:6-11; Heb 5:8-10). He also taught the same for us (Mk 10:43-45).

AN END TO DEATH

Death, our inevitable earthly demise, is the sign for most of us of utter meaninglessness. It is the end of all our plans, those of the present and those we would like to continue to experience in the future as we live out our human existence. The darkness of what awaits us, the unknown which in death reaches its peak through fear of what is beyond, and our lack of faith and hope in God's caring love and the truth of His revelation all compound the sense of the utter finality and meaninglessness of our death.

But the daily deaths that we are called upon to embrace all work unto good if we love the Lord (Rm 8:28). They may bring to us certain doubts at times, it is true, as to whether we can find meaning, purpose, enrichment, growth in such evident negative diminishments—unless we have deep faith. All of us tend more readily to believe in the worldly principle: the more we give away of our riches, our lives, ourselves in love, the less we end up with. This is not the Gospel revelation that insists that to give up all out of loving service is to possess all. Lose your life and you will gain it.

Jesus on the cross preeminently faced meaninglessness. He had to pass over from darkness into the glory of His resurrection by believing that love is most created in such darkness and in the dispossession of one's very life. For this reason the Father raised Him up in glory (Ph 2:9). We dilute the true meaning of the Good News about Christ's resurrection when we picture merely that His soul returned to His dead body. That is resuscitation and not resurrection unto a new creation (Rv 1:18).

This new creation, by our Baptism, is extended to us. We can now share in the victory of Jesus Christ over sin and death. We can now share in His resurrectional glory as we surrender to Christ's lordship and live by love for others and no longer for ourself.

> And for anyone who is in Christ, there is a new creation; the old creation has gone, and now the new one is here. It is all God's work. It was God who reconciled us to himself through Christ and gave us the work of handing on this reconciliation. In other words, God in Christ was reconciling the world to himself, not holding men's faults against them, and he has entrusted to us the news that they are reconciled (2 Cor 5:17-19).

We have been freed from slavery to sin as Jesus applies to us the fruits of His resurrection: ". . . Jesus who was put to death for our sins and raised to life to justify us" (Rm 4:25). We now share in His eternal life because Jesus "died and was raised to life" (2 Cor 5:15). If we cannot share in His resurrection even now, then ". . . you are still in your sins" (1 Cor 15:17).

An outstanding scripture scholar, Ernst Käsemann, insists that the glory of Christ is extended to His followers so they can even now share in His death and resurrection:

> For Paul the glory of Jesus consists in the fact that he makes his disciples on earth willing and capable to bear the cross after him, and the glory of the Church and of Christian life consists in the fact that they have the honor of glorifying the crucified Christ as the wisdom and power of God, to seek salvation in him alone, and to let their lives become a service to God under the sign of Golgotha. The theology of the resurrection is at this point a chapter in the theology of the cross, not its supersession.[1]

RETURN TO MYSTERY

The mystery of the resurrection lies in the mystery of God's love as experienced through the Spirit that the risen

Jesus releases in our heart to know the love of God as seen through the death of Christ for each one of us. Love begets love. This mystery can never be proved by rational arguments. The message of the Good News is that we share now in Christ's resurrection by experiencing God's infinite love for us in Christ's suffering. This experience, which is an ongoing process in contemplative prayer, produces the degree of our sharing in Christ's resurrection by the fruit produced as we manifest love for those around us.

The work of the risen Jesus is to release His Spirit. We are to extend our first Baptism of water into a continued Baptism through Christ risen in His Spirit of love. Now the risen Jesus can pour out the living waters of life upon each one of us (Jn 7:38). St. Paul could boldly claim that if the Spirit of Jesus raised Him to a new life, so that same Spirit now can raise us also into a sharing of His eternal, glorious life.

> . . . the Spirit of God has made his home in you. . . . Though your body may be dead it is because of sin, but if Christ is in you then your spirit is life itself because you have been justified: and if the Spirit of him who raised Jesus from the dead is living in you, then he who raised Jesus from the dead will give life to your own mortal bodies through his Spirit living in you (Rm 8:9-11).

Already by the Spirit of Jesus each of us is a child of God, an heir of Heaven and a co-heir with Christ forever (Rm 8:17; Gal 4:6). If we share the life of Christ in us through the Spirit, then we already share in His resurrection and in His glory as we choose to embrace the cross of suffering which our false self necessarily brings into our life when we seek to live by true love and not by selfishness. There will always be sufferings if we are to live in the life of the Spirit of the risen Jesus and to bring forth the fruit of the Spirit that is love, peace, joy, gentleness, kindliness, patience and forebearance (Gal 5:22).

APPLICATIONS TO OUR DAILY LIFE

The applications of living our share in death-resurrection at each moment of our human situation are innumerable. The Spirit convinces us now of our inner dignity and beauty as a child of God. Each of us is a child of the light and we no longer wish to walk in darkness. Jesus' truth, that He is true God and true man, who has died for love of us to image the burning love of our Heavenly Father, is setting us free in this given moment as we choose to be who we are. We are no longer under the law: the Spirit of the risen Jesus has set us free. In that dignity and inner freedom we stand attentive and guard every thought, word and deed. We bring into captivity and under obedience to Jesus Christ every thought and every desire (2 Cor 10:5).

True love is always self-emptying in loving service toward the one loved. Obedience to Christ is the index of our love for Him. And the degree that we have died to our self-centeredness indicates the measure of our loving union with Him. Jesus has said that if we truly love Him, we will keep His word "and my Father will love him, and we shall come to him and make our home with him" (Jn 14:23). Keeping Christ's word, which he continually speaks within us (and we recognize it through His Spirit), goes beyond observing only the ten commandments and even beyond the teachings found in the New Testament. His Spirit brings us into an intimacy with Christ that comes down to a state of listening always to the indwelling Voice as He reveals to us the mind of the Father in each event and how the Father would wish us to act, think and speak in this moment according to our unique being in Christ that has always been loved eternally by the Father in Him. Our greatest desire is to listen to and obey the voice of Jesus out of love for the Father.

Abandonment to the triune God that dwells within us is the freest act of love we can make and we strive to live in this surrendering act at all times. Its essence is a joyful renunciation of all self-centeredness in order to do what we perceive by our mind, enlightened by grace, to be pleasing to God.

St. Paul describes our life hidden in the risen Lord:

> Since you have been brought back to true life with Christ, you must look for the things that are in heaven, where Christ is, sitting at God's right hand. Let your thoughts be on heavenly things, not on the things that are on the earth, because you have died, and now the life you have is hidden with Christ in God. But when Christ is revealed—and he is your life—you too will be revealed in your glory with him (Col 3:1-4).

LIVING IN CHRIST

Our life now is lived more and more consciously as a oneness in love with Christ. We live no longer for ourselves but Christ Jesus lives in us (Gal 2:19-20) and directs us from within. We put on His values, His "mind," by a constant inner revolution (Ep 4:17).

In all moments we believe He is our Lord and Master who by His resurrection has been given full power over all creatures in heaven and on earth. He is inserted by His resurrection into every atom of matter and is recapitulating the entire cosmos back to the Father unto its fulfillment as the Father originally planned it all to be in Christ and for Christ.

". . . for in him were created all things in heaven and on earth; everything visible and everything invisible . . . and all things [are] to be reconciled through him and for him, everything in heaven and everything on earth, when he made peace by his death on the cross" (Col 1:15-20).

Each one of us is called with our God-given talents and charisms in our own state of life in the context of our own human situation in the universe where we have been placed by God's providence in time and space to help in this great process of the christification of the universe. He calls us to be a reconciler also of the whole world (2 Cor 5:18). Our daily work, our very thoughts and words, all can be directed unto this glorious unification of all things unto God's glory, a beginning of living already in Heaven.

WILL WE RISE FROM THE DEAD?

Will we rise from the dead at the end of the world? Yes, this is the Christian belief. It is the Church's way of emphasizing the fullness, the *pleroma* of all creatures at the end of the world taking their place in the unification of the Body of Christ. But we have already entered into this process of sharing even now in the resurrection of Jesus. How difficult it is for us, who have grown up with an objectivized concept of our own final resurrection as a union of our two parts, a return of our soul into our earthly body, to understand the more biblical concept from which St. Paul is working. The importance of overcoming the limitations of a Platonic concept of "body" to put on a more holistic and more biblical concept is stressed by the theologian and Pauline scholar, Maurice Carrez, in a quote worthy of our attention, even if it is a bit long:

> For Paul the body cannot be reduced simply to the material component of the animated being which is man. It is enough to read, for example, 1 Cor 6:13-7:4; 12:12-27; 15:35-44 to gain an idea of what the body is: it makes possible the human existence willed by God; it expresses the possibilities of man's life; it allows sexual union and commits the whole being that it is and represents; it is the human person in his entirety, his identification, his reality with all its activities, its values; it is not merely one element among many; the word "body" rather describes man in a definite situation, in relation to others, than reduced to himself alone, rather than placed in a dynamism

which makes him live with others, expresses his existence with its possibilities and its brief span, rather than man considered as static. The body is man responsible for what he does, for how he lives; it is his entire situation, his totality, his personality.[2]

What now is stressed in such a biblical vision of the resurrection of the body is that each of us, as a unique personality being formed now in our relationships with others in this earthly existence, will continue to unfold, giving us our identity in and through our "body," our entire, unique personality. Our "body," as fully risen in the life to come, is being shaped and formed now as we share in the risen "body" of Christ by dying to selfishness and living in Him.

This process began in our first "death," Baptism. After our final death we will take possession of our new oneness in Christ and at the end of the world in the general resurrection we will come into a new oneness in Christ as we will then share more fully in the glorification of Christ the Head and all the members—from the beginning of time until the last human being on the face of the earth—who make up, through loving obedience to Him, His Body, the Church.

This is the meaning of St. Paul's statement that in Baptism we Christians are buried with Christ and "by Baptism, too, you have been raised up with him through your belief in the power of God who raised him from the dead" (Col 2:12). Even now, St. Paul insists, by taking away our sins and bringing us to life with Christ, God "raised us up with him and gave us a place with him in heaven, in Christ Jesus" (Ep 2:5-6).

The final resurrection is important but only as a gathering together of the entire Body of Christ in a great cosmic exaltation of those who have already shared in a lifetime of living in His resurrection. Jesus holds out to us even now a share in that resurrection as He tells us through Martha:

I am the resurrection.
If anyone believes in me, even though he dies he will live,
and whoever lives and believes in me
will never die.
Do you believe this? (Jn 11:25-26).

RESURRECTION—AN EVOLVING PROCESS

Our resurrection is, therefore, an evolving process, an unfolding of the life of the Trinity, given in our Baptism when we were first inserted into the Body of the risen Christ, the Head. Christ, historically the same person born of Mary who died on the cross, rose from the dead. His resurrectional "body" was not a separated part that had died and in the resurrection was reunited to the soul. The whole person, Jesus Christ, was raised in glory by the Father into a new existence.

Our "body" will also rise from the dead. We are not given a detailed description of this mystery, how it will happen and what our "body" will look like. But we will be "copies of his glorious body" (Ph 3:21). St. Paul over and over insists on the process of the *already* and the *not yet* of the resurrection as experienced by us humans. The whole person dying in Christ will be raised up and given a glorious body. But we should remember that for St. Paul this means the whole person, each of us as an individuated and recognized human personality sharing, in some mysterious way that Paul cannot describe, the glorified life of Christ. He hints at it when he writes: ". . . the thing that is sown is perishable but what is raised is imperishable; the thing that is sown is contemptible but what is raised is glorious; the thing that is sown is weak but what is raised is powerful; when it is sown, it embodies the soul, when it is raised it embodies the spirit" (1 Cor 15:42-44).

It is always by way of analogies that we approach the mystery of our own resurrection and how we will appear. "The

Lord God will be shining on them." . . . "We shall be like him because we shall see him as he really is" (Rv 22:5; 1 Jn 3:2).

What is of the utmost importance in our consideration of our own resurrection from the dead is to realize that in this *now* moment lies the decision already to live, not so as to receive in the life to come, but already to share in Christ's glorious resurrection, as we keep His commands to love God with our whole heart and our neighbor as ourselves.

FINAL GLORY

We believe as Christians (through the constant teaching of the Church as it interprets God's revealed Word in Scripture) that, as there will be an end to our earthly and material, bodily existence, so also there will come an end to the material world that surrounds us. God never creates matter to be destroyed or annihilated but only to be transformed, to come into a greater harmony that will reflect in an ongoing process for all eternity God's infinite glory and beauty refracted in His multiplicity of creatures.

We believe that not merely those who have lived intimately in the Spirit of the Body of Christ will be "saved" but the entire cosmos will come into a unity of fulfillment at the end of the world. How this will take place has not been revealed to us by God in detail. What has been revealed to us is our mutual responsibility to add to the coming of the final glory of the universe in Christ. Even now we are to bring, by our creative work and involvement in God's created world, some degree of movement of this world toward the fullness of the Body of Christ. You and I have a unique role to play that no one else can play in the same way to bring the world to completion.

This necessitates living consciously in Christ as we are directed individually and guided by His Spirit in all we do. Our own individual resurrection into the newness of life as we share the resurrection of Christ, and our contribution to raise the world into a greater oneness in Christ, both depend on our dying daily to our selfishness (which alone brings about separation and division, disharmony and disunity within ourselves and within the world around us).

CHRIST'S SECOND COMING

Such a dynamic vision of our own individual resurrection and the united resurrection into glory of the entire world into the Body of Christ changes our vision of the second coming of Christ. His victory and glorious triumph at the end of the world will be tied to the cooperation of each and every human being. Christian redemption ultimately means that the entire cosmos is to be transformed into Christ. St. Paul sees the breathtaking vision of the cosmic Christ only at the end of his earthly life as he summarizes it: "There is only Christ; he is everything and he is in everything" (Col 3:11).

The Good News is that Christ is already coming and is here now accomplishing this fuller coming through you and me, members of His Body, the Church. Images and questions of what Christ will look like when He comes to "rapture" us into glory and take us out of the damned world only put off our responsibility to recognize that the anti-Christ spirit is already in our hearts and around us in the world. Yet we are called also to proclaim and act on the paschal victory of Christ who lives in us.

He is coming by our discovery of Him already here whenever we perform an act of love on behalf of His brethren (Mt 25). When we love one another His love is being released and perfected in this world (1 Jn 4:12). There is really a resurrection of our body and also of the materiality of the entire world as the total world is recognized in love as forming the glorified Christ. It is presently being fulfilled as we pass judgment on ourselves and opt to live in Christ and for Christ by living for others in loving service.

DYNAMIC LIVING NOW

We are always searching as frantic hunters to find meaningfulness in our lives while we journey on this earth. At times we might think it is all in our minds, the way we see things, and hence we attend seminars and read "how-to" books to increase our psychic powers. All too often such attempts can only increase our slavery to our false selves as we selfishly seek to become powerful within ourselves, and not humbly live in loving service to others.

A static view of Heaven, Hell and Purgatory can also help us to put off dynamically living now by holding out to us a future, objectivized Heaven awaiting those who obey the laws of God and live by the doctrines taught by the Church. In such a vision this life is a drag, and we must endure life patiently until death comes sweetly to take us home. Such a view of life after death can be loaded with selfishness, perpetuating the security that our religion perhaps gave us, enabling us to avoid the words of Christ: "If anyone wants to be a follower of mine, let him renounce himself and take up his cross and follow me. For anyone who wants to save his life will lose it; but anyone who loses his life for my sake will find it" (Mt 16:24-25).

Jesus in the Gospel is not very much concerned with details about the end of the world or what we will look like upon our resurrection. He is calling us daily to a decision in the present *now* moment to live completely for God and one another. The question of our resurrection and our eternal life in glory is tied to our effective living of Christ's teaching about the cross and death in a loving self-sacrifice. Any other way is a selfish cop-out extending a "spiritualized" selfishness into eternity. True maturity is to live for the entire cosmos, the entire Body of Christ that God called into being through His Word. But that Word cannot be spoken in all its completion unless with Mary, the Mother of the Word of God, we daily utter *our* "fiat": "Be it done unto me according to thy word."

PRAYER TO THE RISEN LORD

Lord Jesus, I come before You this day in all my brokenness and frailty. In my present mood and life-situation I am much closer to Your passion and death than I am to Your resurrection. I wonder how any good can come out of the entanglements of my life that seem at the present moment to be a moving blanket of darkness that ever so gradually is approaching to cover me and suffocate in me any breath of life.

How can I, Divine Savior, ever believe that an eternal life awaits me beyond the seeming "no-sense" of this present life? How can I ever believe that I will rise from the final death that will suck out my last breath and send me into the dark unknown?

Yet, as I stretch out to You in prayer I feel like your two disciples on the road to Emmaus. How they, too, found it so incredible to believe that You, Lord Jesus, should have suffered such an ignominious death on the cross. And still You were risen from the dead. You patiently taught them from Scripture of the necessity that You had to die in order to enter into a new existence of glory.

I can hear You saying to me those same words: "You foolish men! So slow to believe the full message of the prophets! Was it not ordained that the Christ should suffer and so enter into his glory?" (Lk 24:25-26). How slow I am to believe that out of the brokenness and meaninglessness of my present life a new and glorious life can follow! Even slower am I to believe that I can even now, as I choose to act in love by putting on Your mind, share in your glorious resurrection.

Teach me, Master, that, as I live in the power of Your paschal victory now, I am already sharing in a new life that will continue to grow "from glory to glory" until the final resurrection when You will come in full glory to manifest Yourself in Your Body, Your members, including myself, as the fully risen Christ, uniting all in the fullness of Your resurrection.

May I learn as You did on the cross how "to obey through suffering" (Heb 5:8). May I have new eyes to see You coming in the *now* moment of my brokenness to lift me to a new sharing in Your resurrection. Resurrection is *now*, Lord, as I humbly accept to die to my isolated selfishness in order to let You in all Your risen power lead me to a sharing in our oneness with the entire creation through our oneness in You.

Death can have no hold over me as I live in the daily belief of Your power to lift me out of darkness into Your eternal life. I thank You for Your revelation and Your continued actualizing in my life of St. Paul's prayer of victory:

> Death is swallowed up in victory.
> Death, where is your victory?
> Death, where is your sting? . . .
> So let us thank God for giving
> us the victory through our Lord Jesus Christ (1 Cor 15:55-57).

Footnotes

1. Ernst Käsemann, "The Pauline Theology of the Cross," in *Interpretation*, Vol. XXIV, no. 2, p. 177; cited by Lloyd Geering, *Resurrection: A Symbol of Hope* (London: Hodder & Stoughton, 1971).
2. Maurice Carrez, "With What Body Do the Dead Rise Again?" in *Immortality and Resurrection*, Vol. 60 of *Concilium* (N.Y.: Paulist Press, 1970), p. 93.